W<small>E</small>

"There are moments that ... m and define who they become. This is the story of one woman's journey of defying that brokenness and finding hope to overcome. If you've ever wondered if God can restore a life then read Linda's story and discover for yourself what He can do. Her story will inspire you to believe that anything is possible when God shows up."

Joel Enyart
Lead Pastor
Redwood Park Church

"What an honour to read Linda's life story. She is a shining example of survival and resilience. I hope the book will inspire hope for those suffering abuse, and serve as a cautionary tale for those that counsel and support sufferers of abuse."

Maurice Fortin,
C.E.O., Canadian Mental Health Association, (retired)
Thunder BayBranch

"Her story is a testament to God's faithfulness, to the church's role as a place for healing, and the power that comes through sharing *story*."

C. David Donaldson,
author of *Don't Sing Another Man's Song,*
Mission of Mercenary, and *Courage of Grace*

The Life of Linda Stewardson

THE
GIRL WHO
WOULDN'T DIE

Marianne Jones
with Linda Stewardson

THE GIRL WHO WOULDN'T DIE
Copyright © 2015 by Marianne Jones

While the events in this story are true, some names and places have been changed to protect the identities of the people involved.

ISBN: 978-1-4866-1116-4

Word Alive Press
131 Cordite Road, Winnipeg, MB R3W 1S1
www.wordalivepress.ca

WORD ALIVE
—PRESS—

Cataloguing in Publication may be obtained through Library and Archives Canada

This book is dedicated to Dr. Harvey Armstrong, who believed in me long before I believed in myself, and to all the innocent children who have been victimized.

—Linda Stewardson

CONTENTS

FOREWORD

The story you are about to read is important. It is a book about courage, resilience, strength, and determination. It also demonstrates that these characteristics can carry a human being through a hellish childhood to a successful adulthood. Linda blossomed into a great wife, a wonderful mother, and an outstanding contributor to her own community. Linda's story illustrates many aspects of the impact of abuse and neglect of children, which is the most important and preventable contributor to negative life consequences.

Linda's story foundered on ignorance and the lack of curiosity of others. It also foundered in the disbelief that she encountered when she tried to tell her story. Our society's inability to hear, accept, and support abused children is well documented in the United States' Centers for Disease Control's Aversive Childhood Experiences (ACE) Study, which records the physical health, mental health, social deviance, educational failures, criminal justice, marital, and parenting problems that victims experience. Abuse and neglect impact very large numbers of people. They also cost more than any other cause of human distress.

Linda's experiences illustrate the blindness and deafness of many social, healthcare, and justice professionals when it comes to the incidence and impact of child abuse and neglect. Many do not want to know. I have had professional contact with thousands of people who were abused and neglected as children. Most of them who visited professionals in the hope of getting help were not asked about previous abuse. If the patient or client disclosed the abuse, they were either disbelieved, as Linda was, or rejected and punished. Sometimes the helper added to the harm by having sex with or bullying the survivor. It is easier to disbelieve than to involve oneself in the length and depth of relationship required to restore trust and the capacity to experience secure attachment.

Since I became aware of the prevalence of child abuse and neglect and its impact, along with many others, I have come to realize that this is one of our society's best kept secrets. In my own life, it turned out that my wife Mary experienced abuse from family members while she was a young child. Mary dissociated the experiences, and then with good help remembered them and recovered. She recounts the process in her own book, *Confessions of a Trauma Therapist: A Memoir of Healing and Transformation.*

Without Mary's love and support, I could not have extended my care of Linda as much as I did. It was obvious to both of us that for Linda to recover her life and heal her wounds, I had to do many things I could never do for most patients. In return, Linda was, without knowing it, becoming an excellent teacher about the effects of trauma and how to help minimize its impact. I also learned from being the clinical director and director of a maximum security hospital and crisis service for dangerous and ill teens, where many of the young people had never previously disclosed abuse. Being a member of two task forces confronting abuse of patients by health care providers added to what my patients taught me.

My formal teachers in medicine and psychiatry taught me almost nothing about child abuse and its impact. The medical students and psychiatric residents I taught knew very little about the incidence and impact, despite the fact that it is far more common than the syndromes they had been taught to recognize and treat. I hope some of them read this story and learn some of the painful truths Linda discloses.

As I read the manuscript, I was drawn back to the times and episodes we shared. My eyes filled with tears as I remembered some of her suffering, while she remembered what had happened to her and understood its impact. I was not a part of Linda's early life, so I cannot vouch for the veracity of what she says about it. I can, however, vouch for the events that happened after her mid-teens. There were many more horrible events that she excluded from the story, as there were too many of them, and they would have distracted from the theme of the book. I am thankful to her maternal grandmother, who I theorize managed to help Linda develop some sense of security before the aneurysm took her away from her.

I feel honoured and privileged to be asked to write this foreword. It is a reward for having travelled so far with Linda. When I met her, she stood at the door of my office in Youthdale, afraid to come in and sit down. I recognized the sexualized fear in her eyes and body, and asked the appropriate questions. She told me who, where, and when she had been abused. I told her that I would help her if she ever confronted her main perpetrators. I recognized her intelligence, goodness, and the beauty inside her. After another suicide attempt, I admitted her to the maximum security unit, and discharged her after a couple of weeks during which I got to know her better. She came to see me more often, and she began to request help with many problems. I helped her deal with several suicide attempts that were nearly fatal.

As I came to know her better, she began to expose her other ego states to me. Some were seductive, some were aggressive, and others could not believe that I would never sexualize her, hurt her, exploit her, or give up on her. The honour of writing this foreword comes from her entire being deciding that I was caring and reliable. Thank you, Linda, for trusting and attaching, and for the faith that carried you forward when nothing else worked for you.

—Dr. Harvey Armstrong, M.D., F.R.C.P.(C)

INTRODUCTION

When I first heard Linda Stewardson share her astonishing story, I was transfixed. I knew that it was a book waiting to be written. When I approached her later, explaining that I was a writer and asking if she was interested in working on a manuscript with me, it was the beginning of a friendship as well as a partnership. Linda is the real deal. She has survived a childhood that would have destroyed most people and become a healthy, generous person who radiates love and joy.

This book has truly been a labour of love for both of us. It has been an honour for me to have a part in telling Linda's story. It is our sincere prayer that it will bring hope to many who suffer from the wounds of abuse and addiction.

—Marianne Jones

"WHY DID YOU STAB YOURSELF?"

CHAPTER ONE

I OPENED MY EYES TO THE WHITE WALLS OF A HOSPITAL ROOM.
Confused, and in terrible pain from the wounds in my chest, I saw standing in the doorway the person I feared most in the world: Gerry, my stepfather. The man who had just tried to kill me.

What was he doing there? Why was I still alive? Panic filled me. I looked away and stared at the wall, too terrified to even look at him.

"So you're finally awake," a doctor standing at my bedside said. He told me that a man had found me lying on the beach beside a remote lake and had brought me to the hospital a few hours before. Then he asked me an unbelievable question: "Why did you stab yourself?"

I wondered if I had heard him correctly,

Is he crazy? I thought. *Does he actually think I did this to myself?*

I was totally confused, not understanding what was going on around me.

Suddenly Gerry was talking, telling me that I was very lucky I had missed my heart. He said he had found my journal entry where I had written that I was going to kill myself.

I felt disoriented, unable to take in what was happening. It was true that I had written in my journal a few months before that I wanted to die. After years of enduring beatings and rape from Gerry, I felt desperate, with nowhere to turn. But how could any sane adult believe that a thirteen-year-old girl could stab herself six times in the chest with a filleting knife? Why did no one ask how I had gotten to that isolated lake on my own?

With Gerry standing there, I was too terrified to answer the doctor. I stared at the ceiling in silence, not contradicting Gerry's version of events.

I felt totally helpless and hopeless—that there was no way out of the situation. I wanted my mom. Gerry asked me why I was crying. I said it was because I wanted my mom.

Once before I had tried to tell the truth about what was happening at home, to my teacher. Mr. H. was a fun teacher who joked around with us a lot and never got angry. He gave us movie days every Friday and often brought bags of candy and popcorn for the class.

I often looked depressed and put my head down on my desk. Mr. H. noticed and would say, "Linda, what's wrong? Is something going on?"

One Friday, I was really scared. That morning, Gerry had said he would be going to the beer store. I knew that this meant beatings and rape waited for me when I got home. Worried and preoccupied, I was having trouble concentrating or doing my work in class. At recess I was sitting by myself, and Mr. H. came over and asked me if anything was wrong. I confided that I was afraid to go home.

"Why?" Mr. H. said.

"Because I think my dad is drinking," I answered.

"Why would that scare you?"

"Because my dad gets really, really angry when he's drinking, and hurts me."

"Don't worry," Mr. H. assured me. "Everything will be okay. I'll get back to you."

For the rest of the day I kept glancing at the classroom clock, wondering if Mr. H. had arranged for someone to talk to me. I hoped so. I was really afraid to go home. But no one came. At the end of the day, I got on the bus with my brother Brian and rode the long ride home.

As soon as I walked in the door, Gerry was waiting for me, belt in hand.

"You know I told you what would happen if you ever told anybody," he said.

He beat me so severely that I could only curl up in pain afterward. I felt as though it was my own fault for telling on Gerry. I would never make that mistake again.

On Monday, Mr. H. asked me to stay behind at recess so that he could talk to me. He said that he wanted to take me somewhere that evening where there were people who could help me. I phoned home and told my parents that I was going out on an outing with my youth group after school.

I stayed in the classroom at the end of the school day as my classmates got on the bus. Mr. H. drove me to North Bay, chatty and joking all the way. I assumed that he was taking me to a doctor's office. Instead he pulled up in front of a small church on Main Street. We went inside and down to the basement. The room was dark, with candles lit and a group of six or seven adults in black gowns. I saw another girl from my class there, sitting on a chair in the corner.

I was petrified. I had no idea what was going on. I wondered if this was some kind of church ceremony.

I saw someone take a knife and slit the throats of some birds. They poured the blood into a cup and passed it around and everyone drank from it. Then they told me to get on a table in the centre. Two men assaulted me. I could hear people chanting and laughing as this was going on. The other girl was crying in the corner.

I remember screaming on the inside. I blacked out.

When it was over, they told me to get dressed. One of the men, Lorenzo, gave me a phone number. He said that if I knew of any other kids who I thought would come to their meetings, to call and let him know.

Mr. H. drove me home in silence. The only time he spoke was to warn me not to say anything about what had happened or he would tell my stepfather what I had said about him. That was a meaningless threat, since I figured he had already told Gerry on Friday. But I had no intention of saying anything anyway, since adults clearly weren't safe to confide in.

The other girl and I saw each other at school every day after that, and acted normal. We never spoke about what had happened. But for some reason I never forgot the phone number Lorenzo had given me. It seemed to be etched in my memory.

One thing I was sure of: I would never reach out to anyone for help again, and I would never trust any adult or authority figure. So no matter how much the doctor might try to get me to answer his questions, I refused to speak.

I spent six months in the hospital being visited by people from the psychiatric ward because of my supposed suicide attempt. Gerry visited me regularly, to all appearances the concerned stepfather. The truth was, he came to remind me to keep my mouth shut. He was afraid that if he stayed away, someone at the hospital might get me to open up and start talking.

He didn't have to worry. I knew that if I ever said anything, I would be dead.

Doug, the neighbour who had discovered me on the beach, came to visit once. He told me that he had found me in a garbage bag and had feared the worst. When he realized I was still breathing, he had rushed me to the hospital.

With six stab wounds in my chest, it seemed a miracle that I was still alive. Gerry told me during one of those hospital visits, "I wish I had gotten you in the heart."

To this day I don't understand how the doctor could have asked me why I had tried to stab myself—or how I could have been discharged from the hospital without an investigation. It seems unbelievable that nobody—not the doctor, the police, the school principal who had seen Gerry pull me out of school that day, or the neighbour who found me—ever questioned Gerry's story that I had tried to commit suicide. Did they seriously believe that I had stabbed myself multiple times before climbing into a garbage bag? They must have had suspicions. After all, Mattawa was so small that everyone knew each other's business. If I so much as climbed a tree, my parents heard about it before I got home.

Still, no one investigated any further. Gerry was well-known in Mattawa. Maybe it was just easier not to ask too many questions.

Hopelessness and helplessness engulfed me. My prayers to be set free from Gerry's abuse seemed to go unanswered. Nobody in town would help. Even my mother was silent and made no effort to protect me. She was too afraid of Gerry, who beat her regularly.

For years I had lain in bed at night listening to my mother screaming and crying while Gerry punched her in the face and pulled her hair. I would put my pillow over my face to quiet my sobs, hoping and praying that he would stop before he killed her. I desperately longed to rescue my mother from the hands of this madman, but I knew I was no match for him.

Gerry's rage wasn't limited to me and my mom. He often beat the four younger children with a belt, or picked them up by the ears and shook them while they were kicking and screaming in the air. Many times he dropped baby Ian on his head. But I was the one he had been molesting every night since he'd moved in with us when I was eight. He would tell me that if I told, no one would believe me and I would be taken away from home and locked up forever—if he didn't kill me first.

I had good reason to take his threats seriously. Sometimes he beat me so severely that I was convinced he would kill me one day, and there was nothing I could do to stop it from happening.

After the beatings, I would go to my room and crawl under my blankets in a ball, wishing I would just go to sleep and never wake up. Dying couldn't possibly be any worse than what I was experiencing here in this world.

How did my life get to be such a nightmare? It hadn't always been like this. There had once been a time when I had felt happy and loved.

"PLEASE, GOD, NOT MY GRANDMA!"

CHAPTER TWO

Up until I was six years old, my younger brother Brian and I were raised by our grandmother.

Grandma was tall, with black, curly hair. My memories of her are few, but very positive and filled with love. She was a kind-hearted, devout Baptist. She made it her mission in life to spoil me with mounds of ice cream and soda pop, and you never heard any complaints from me! She owned an organ, which she played often. I never knew what she was playing, but the music sounded beautiful to my ears.

Our grandparents owned a small country restaurant and lived downstairs. I remember customers dropping in every day to chat and make purchases, but it wasn't what you'd call busy.

My brother and I amused ourselves playing outside. I remember a wooden shed in the back with an attached clothesline. Brian and I had fun climbing up and jumping on the shed.

There was a storage room downstairs where supplies for the restaurant were kept. The door was usually latched, but one day it happened to be off the hook. I accidentally pulled the door onto myself and all the cans of food fell on me. Grandma drove me to the hospital where they stitched me up. I still have a small scar on my mouth from that incident.

Every night Grandma would tuck us into bed, saying, "Don't forget to say your prayers."

The Christmas Day when I was six, our lives changed forever. I will always remember that day. The house was full of people, including my cousins, and my mother, who visited occasionally. There was the usual fun and excitement of presents, a tree, and special food.

Suddenly, I heard sirens. Men in uniforms appeared at our door with a stretcher, and carried Grandma out into a waiting ambulance. She had collapsed with what we later learned was a ruptured aneurysm.

I stood in a corner of the room, tears running down my face. I thought Grandma was dying. I kept thinking, *Please God, not my grandma. I love her so much!*

After Grandma was taken away, I prayed daily that God would bring her back to me. I didn't really understand who God was, but Grandma had told me that God lived in the sky and could hear my prayers. I believed Grandma because she never lied, so I prayed harder than ever. I pleaded with God to please make Grandma well again and bring her back. I couldn't imagine a life without the one person I truly came to love.

But Grandma never came home. She was destined to spend the remaining thirty years of her life in the hospital.

Shortly after Grandma was hospitalized, Mom came for us. I couldn't remember ever living with our mom in the past. She seemed more like an acquaintance, an occasional visitor at our grandparents' home. I thought that this new living situation was just a temporary one.

I continued to pray. There was no doubt in my mind that God was listening to my prayers. He knew how much I missed Grandma. He would bring her back to me.

I remember crying one night at bedtime because I missed Grandma so much. My mom was very cold about it. She said that tears wouldn't bring Grandma back.

Mom would get snappy with me whenever I asked when Grandma was coming back. "God took your grandmother," she would say, "so ask Him to bring her back." Other times she would say that Grandma was gone for good. "She's never coming back, so you'd better get used to the idea that you're going to be living with me for a long time."

I thought that God wasn't so nice because He had taken the only person I loved away from me.

Mom was living with a man named Charles, with whom she had two other children, Katy and Doug. Brian and I shared a bedroom in our new family's apartment. We missed the restaurant and yard, but there were friends in the building to play with and tricycles to ride in the neighbourhood.

I remember a conversation I had with Brian when I was seven or eight. We were talking about Grandma and what we would do if either of us ever had an aneurysm. He said that he wouldn't let anyone operate on his head, that he would rather just go to heaven. This conversation came back to me years later.

Grandpa often came to visit, paying special attention to me. He loved to spoil me. He always remembered my birthday and brought a nice gift. He never made such a fuss about the other kids. He was so nice to me that I didn't understand why there was so much tension between him and Mom. The two of them argued whenever he came to visit, and she never wanted to talk about him. All she would say was that he had been very strict when she was a child. That didn't seem to explain the unease between the two of them.

I don't remember Charles very well. The only things I do remember were that he was an alcoholic, and that he and Mom were constantly fighting and screaming at each other. I woke up almost every night crying because I could hear them fighting. Brian and I missed the quiet peace and beautiful music of Grandma's home. But there was much worse ahead.

After two years of this arrangement, I woke up to the familiar sounds of Mom and Charles arguing loudly. The next thing I knew, Mom came storming into the bedroom. She got all of us out of bed, lined us up in the living room, and told us that she and Charles were going their separate ways. She said that two of us would have to go with Charles, and the other two could stay with her. Then she looked at me and said that since I was the oldest, I could choose first.

I stood there, unsure what to do, having no idea which of them I wanted to live with. After much deliberation, I chose Mom. Brian, the second oldest, did the same.

Katy and Doug were left with Charles. It didn't register with me what had just happened until I saw Katy and Doug leaving with

Charles. My eyes began to sting. Where were they going? Would I ever see them again?

I thought about praying, but then thought, *Why bother? God didn't bring Grandma back. Why should I think that He'll bring Katy and Doug back? God is probably just some fairy tale Grandma told me.*

Shortly after that, Mom met Gerry. She then decided to get Katy and Doug back. They were living in Nova Scotia at the time with Charles and his parents. Mom left Brian and me with a sitter while she drove to Nova Scotia with Gerry and Grandpa.

I waited, torn between anticipation and fear of disappointment. I missed Katy and Doug, but was excited about reuniting with them. On the other hand, what if Charles refused to let them go?

LIFE WITH GERRY

CHAPTER THREE

WHEN MOM AND GERRY RETURNED A WEEK LATER WITH KATY AND Doug, I was thrilled and amazed, but my joy didn't last long. Mom immediately began fussing over Katy, making a pet of her and spoiling her. For some reason she never paid as much attention to Doug. I became very jealous and resentful. I yearned for my mother's love and attention, but Mom paid little attention to me. She was always busy with Katy. I blamed Katy for that, and began hating her with a passion.

Soon after bringing Katy and Doug home, Mom and Gerry decided to move closer to Gerry's hometown of Eau Claire, in northeastern Ontario. They found a place in the country on the outskirts of town. The closest neighbours were a quarter-mile away.

They moved in on Halloween night. After they had finished moving all their belongings into the farmhouse, Mom went for a walk. Gerry began fondling me and Katy, telling us that we were playing a tickling game that would be our secret. He warned us not to tell anyone.

I didn't understand what was happening. I was only eight and Katy was six. It was only the beginning of many of these "games" I would be forced to endure.

Like Charles, Gerry was an alcoholic. We learned quickly to stay out his way if his supply of beer ran out. We had a puppy named Lucky, only he wasn't so lucky. One time, in a hurry to drive to the beer store before it closed, Gerry ran over Lucky, killing him instantly. Gerry was furious at the dead puppy for slowing him down in his rush to buy more beer!

What was it about alcohol that could make a person this crazy? I became curious as to why Gerry loved the stuff so much. I started sneaking some out of the cupboards and fridge and drinking it in my closet. I found that it helped me temporarily forget about the abuse. The pain didn't seem so hard to deal with when I was drinking.

The farmhouse we lived in had no inside washroom or running water. I was afraid of going to the outhouse in the middle of the night. Bears weren't an unusual sight on our property. I was petrified of running into a bear in the dark, and equally afraid of waking Gerry. He had been coming into my bedroom at night after my mother had gone to sleep, and fondling me. For both reasons, I always tried to hold on until morning, but would end up wetting the bed instead.

My bedwetting infuriated Gerry. He began checking my bed every morning. If it was wet, he would beat me with a leather belt until I had welts. The beatings got more and more intense and frequent as Gerry's rage at the bedwetting increased. But no matter how I tried or how severely he beat me, I just couldn't seem to help it.

My whole life became one of fear and uncertainty. No matter what I did or how hard I tried not to enrage Gerry, I always found myself at the other end of his belt. He beat me for arguing with my siblings, being sassy, making too much noise in the morning, or for not calling him Dad.

Gerry insisted that I call him Dad, but I refused. In my mind, Gerry would never be my father! I knew that I had a father somewhere, even if I couldn't remember him. I didn't know why he had left us, but I clung to the belief that he loved me and that I would reconnect with him someday. There was no way I was going to let anyone else take his place!

I asked my mother often about my real father. Mom would tell me he was a drug addict and in jail somewhere. I refused to believe it. Every day Gerry beat me for not calling him dad. Still, I would not give in. That made him furious. The beatings became longer and harder at each refusal. One time I counted the number of hits and finally stopped counting at twenty-two.

I never cried in front of Gerry, which made him even angrier. I wasn't going to give him the satisfaction. Instead, I dissociated and shut out the pain. My mind would float away and disappear into a spot on the wall. Although it made it easier to endure the beatings, I could still always see my mother standing in a corner of the room watching. This would make me angry. Why wouldn't she defend me, protect me from this madman? Didn't she love me? Didn't she care?

I felt utterly alone. I was convinced that one day Gerry was going to kill me, and that there was nothing I could do about it.

Afterward, I would go to my room and crawl into bed, gingerly lying on my side, because my back and buttocks were so sore from the whippings. Only then, when I was alone, would I let go and start crying. My mother often came into the room and tried to console me, but I would tell her to leave. I hated Gerry for beating me, but I hated my mother just as much for not protecting me.

When Gerry was particularly angry, he would take me out to the barn, tie my hands to a pole, and horsewhip me. He was always careful to make sure he never struck me in the face so no one would ask questions.

Even then I was stubbornly determined not to give Gerry the pleasure of knowing he had hurt me. I decided that even if he killed me, I wasn't ever going to make a sound. Even if I had screamed at the top of my lungs, our nearest neighbour was a quarter of a mile away. The one thing that enabled Gerry to keep up his savagery was the fact that there was nobody within earshot who might hear and come to my rescue.

I yearned to be able to go to bed at night and not have to worry about the sound of footsteps beside my bed, or to not constantly wonder whether each beating was going to be the one that killed me. At the same time, I came to believe that what was happening was normal, that all my classmates at school were having the same things done to them by their dads. Yet a part of me must have known it wasn't normal, because I often thought about telling Mom what went on every night after she fell asleep.

After giving it a lot of thought, I decided there was no point. I suspected that she already knew, but for some reason was choosing not to protect me. I figured that Mom mustn't love me or care what happened to me.

Every day I walked past the police station on my way to and from school. Sometimes I would think about walking into the station and asking for help. But Gerry had said that if I tried to tell the police, they wouldn't believe me and I would be taken away from home and locked up forever.

Most of the beatings happened when Gerry was drunk, which was pretty much every day. He was rarely sober. On those occasions, the beatings weren't as severe, but life was just as bad, so it didn't make much difference. He would drink every day for a week, take a couple of days to sober up, and then drink for another week. This was a never-ending cycle.

On the days when he was sobering up, he would suffer a severe hangover. He would keep all the lights off in the house, refuse to answer the door or phone, and order all of us kids to stay in bed, unless it was a school day. We were allowed to go to school, but had to go straight to bed as soon as we got home. We weren't allowed to play or talk in bed. If we broke the no-noise rule, he would come in and beat us.

At suppertime we were allowed to come out to eat one at a time, starting with the youngest. Gerry gave us five minutes to eat as much as we could. After five minutes, the rest of our food was thrown out. I learned to eat fast, but not always fast enough. I often went to bed hungry.

Sometimes I would wake up in the middle of the night and tiptoe to the kitchen, looking for something to eat, so ravenous that I didn't care what, as long as it was edible. Usually it was bread and butter. I had to be very careful, trying to open doors while preventing them from squeaking. If I got caught, it meant another beating.

It was around this time that Gerry started taking me for truck rides with his brother-in-law Francois. Francois and his wife would come over to the house to play cards. Afterwards, Gerry and Francois would announce that they were going for a drive, and they would invite me to go with them. I knew I had no choice. Gerry had warned me ahead of time, making it clear that when he asked, saying no wasn't an option.

Sometimes they took me back to Francois' house. Other times they sat in the truck, just around the corner from where they lived. Gerry made me sit between them while they took turns. I was too scared to move or say a word. Gerry would threaten to beat me if I wasn't cooperative. Francois would say it was okay; I didn't have to if I didn't want to. But Gerry was insistent, and I knew better than to refuse.

One time, while this was going on, Mom seemed to come out of nowhere. Gerry saw her approaching and told me to put my clothes on. He and Francois were scrambling with their clothes as she reached the truck. She asked Gerry what they were doing. Gerry said that we were just looking at the stars. She started yelling at me, telling me I had to get home to finish my homework.

I was relieved but very confused. Mom must have suspected what was going on. Couldn't she see them zipping their pants as she was talking to Gerry? It was so obvious; why wouldn't she put a stop to it? Yet the truck rides with the two men continued to go on every few weeks.

School brought a different kind of abuse. Baths were a rarity at our house, since there was no running water. Our only source of income was Gerry`s disability cheque, most of which went towards beer and cigarettes. I was very dirty and poor, and looked it. My clothes were ragged hand-me-downs. None of the other kids wanted to sit with me. I dreaded recess and lunchtime, and games for which kids chose partners or teams. I was always the last one chosen or the only child without a partner. At lunch and recess I stood by myself, watching from a distance while the other kids played marbles, ball, skipping, or baseball. They taunted me, calling me ugly, stinky, potato head. I believed that I was worthless and ugly, and that something was terribly wrong with me.

When I was ten, we moved from Eau Claire to Mattawa, a small town near North Bay, Ontario. Our new home had running water and an inside bathroom. What luxury! My sister Katy and I slept in a double bed in the room across the hall from the room shared by our mother and Gerry. Our brothers shared bunk beds in the living room.

• • •

At the public school, I began making friends for the first time. My best friend was a twelve-year-old girl named Nancy. Finally I had someone with whom to play ball and skip, and go to the beach!

Nancy invited me to Sunday School. The teacher was so nice that I wished she could be my mother. She told us how wonderful God is. She said that God was in control of everything, and that He loved us so much that He gave up his one and only Son to die on a cross just for us.

This was my first knowledge of God's love. It was the love and acceptance I had been yearning for! Grandma had talked about God, but I had been too young at the time to really understand. Now I welcomed Jesus into my heart with a huge sense of relief. All that I had to do now was pray to Him, and He would rescue me and keep me safe from all of Gerry's abuse.

Every day I went home and prayed, never doubting that the God who could do anything would make everything better. However, when nothing changed, I couldn't understand why God wasn't answering me. I felt worthless, not good enough for God to care about.

My newborn faith quickly died and I began to lose all hope. I became angry and bitter, hating God and blaming Him for the daily torture I endured.

If God is in control and is so good, then why did He take my grandmother from me? I thought. *Why doesn't He kill my stepfather and rescue me from his clutches?*

When I was eleven, I began babysitting for our neighbours, Linda and Tom. One time they were going to a weekend party and suggested that I bring my pyjamas and sleep over. After putting their son to bed, I went to bed myself, only to be wakened in the wee hours of the morning, feeling someone lying beside me, trying to take off my underwear. Half-asleep, at first I thought it was Gerry, until I remembered where I was. I sat up and began fighting him off, saying that I wanted to go home. Tom started apologizing and pleaded with me to stay. He promised to leave me alone and sleep in the other room if I would agree to stay. He said that his wife was still at the party and would be home soon.

I wanted to go home, but knew I would have to face Gerry there. I decided that Tom was the lesser of two evils. In the morning, Tom was nowhere to be found. I ate breakfast with Linda, who drove me home.

Gerry was drinking more heavily than ever, and the sexual abuse increased. He would go on five- or six-day binges, and come into my bedroom every night. He would wake Katy and tell her to go into the living room and sleep on the couch.

Pretending to be asleep, I would hope and pray that he would go away and leave me alone. Of course, it was a vain hope.

Afterward, he would say, "Good job, well done," and give me a handful of change, reminding me that this was our little secret. He would tell me that if I told anyone, nobody would believe me and I would be taken away from home and locked up forever—that is, if he didn't kill me first.

Then he would fall asleep in the bed beside me until morning, not leaving until just before Mom woke up.

Around this time, Gerry stopped physically abusing me and began lavishing me with money and treats. Whenever I had an argument with one of my siblings, he would side with me.

One night, when I was eleven, I went to bed with my jeans on under my nightgown, hoping that this would make things difficult for Gerry, so that he would give up. Instead, when he discovered I was wearing my jeans to bed, he ordered me to take them off. When I refused, he grabbed me and hurled me across the room. I crashed into my bike, which was standing in the corner, and the commotion woke Mom. She came running into the bedroom and demanded to know what was going on. Gerry told her that I had gone to bed with my pants on, and that this was very unhealthy for a girl my age.

"Take off your pants," Mom said. "It's unhealthy for you."

Then she went back to bed. Since she was now awake, Gerry followed her. I lay in bed whimpering, covering my head with my pillow to muffle the noise.

Couldn't my mother see what was going on? Didn't she wonder what Gerry was doing in my room at 2:00 a.m.? Didn't she ask him how he had known my jeans were on in the first place?

How could she ask me to take off my clothes the way she did, and then go back to bed? Why wouldn't she protect me and rescue me from this madman?

I cried myself to sleep, my head filled with questions and confusion. Suddenly I was awakened, once again by Gerry. He whispered quietly so as not to wake up my mother.

"The next time you insist on waking your mother, I'm going to get my hunting rifle and shoot you along with your mother and brother and sisters."

I was terrified. I didn't doubt for a minute that he meant business. From that moment on, I decided to stop making any attempt to resist. I became as compliant toward Gerry as a puppy to its master. Whatever he wanted, I would do.

Around this time, I had my first memories of "disappearing," or blanking out. While the abuse was going on, I would stare into a spot in the wall and my mind would disappear into it. Sometimes after Gerry left, I would return to the present and realize that it was over. I just hadn't been present for it. It became my way of surviving.

Sometimes my brother Brian would come up to me and say, "You promised to do such-and-such yesterday." I would have no memory of any such conversation. It was the beginning of my dissociating, but I had very little awareness of it at the time.

I was very excited as my twelfth birthday approached. Even though Mom and Gerry forbade birthday parties or any kind of celebration, I considered this day to be a special one that belonged to me.

That night, Gerry came into my bedroom as always, but this time was different. After sending Katy to sleep in the living room, he latched the bedroom door. He had never done that before, and I sat upright in bed, frightened.

"This is a very special day," Gerry said. "You are now an official tee-nybopper. I am going to give you a birthday gift you'll never forget. Tonight I'm going to make you proud of me by making you into a woman."

Terrified, I lost my innocence and virginity that night. I felt sheer pain going through my whole body until I went numb and lost consciousness.

After he was done, he quickly got up and left without a word. I lay curled in a ball, rocking back and forth, hurting all over. More than anything, I just wanted to die and disappear.

Maybe if I go for a walk in the woods tomorrow, I might be lucky and run into a bear. Even if the bear mauls me to death, it couldn't possibly be as painful as what I'm feeling right now. Someone, PLEASE, I'm begging you to save me!

After that, Gerry's behaviour toward me changed. He became jealous and possessive. He wouldn't allow me to go anywhere where I might run into a guy, which pretty much meant anywhere. School was the only exception. If I even happened to innocently glance at a male, Gerry would slap me across the face and call me a whore and a slut. He would say it was for my own good, to prevent me from running off and eloping or getting pregnant.

That September, Mom had another baby: brother Ian. The first night that she was in the hospital, Gerry spent the night with me.

The next day was one I would remember for the rest of my life.

Since he didn't have to worry about Mom, he told me I wasn't to go to school in the morning with my sisters and brothers. I was angry, knowing that he wanted to take advantage of my mother's absence so that he could use me as his sex slave all day.

I woke up to the sounds of my brothers and sisters making breakfast and getting ready for school. I looked at Gerry. He was sound asleep. Cautiously, I slipped out of bed, so as not to wake him, and joined my brother Brian in the kitchen.

"Do you want to see something real freaky?" I asked. Brian nodded. I led him into my bedroom and pointed at the bed where Gerry lay sprawled naked on his back, snoring. I was desperately hoping that if Brian knew, he would save me. I didn't know how to find the words to tell him, so I showed him instead.

Brian had no idea how to respond to my unspoken plea. He walked out of the room and said, "Let's go to school." Neither of us ever mentioned it again.

Despite Gerry's order, I went to school with my siblings. I hoped to escape Gerry for the day. I soon learned what a mistake that was.

During second period, the principal came into my classroom and up to my desk. He tapped me on the shoulder and said, "Linda, your father is waiting in the parking lot for you. He said you're needed at home."

Terror and panic filled me. Every part of my being wanted to cling to the comfort and safety of my classroom.

Didn't the principal wonder why I had to go home in the middle of the day while all my siblings stayed at school? Couldn't he tell that Gerry was angry and was going to hurt me? Why wouldn't he save me?

But I had no choice. I had to gather my things and go out to face my stepfather.

I went outside, opened the truck door, and climbed into the seat beside Gerry. He drove the mile and a half home without saying a word. I was terrified by his silent fury. When we got home, I walked into the house without daring to speak. He ordered me to take off my clothes and get into bed. I was shaking, thinking, *This is it. Gerry is going to kill me, and there's nobody around to hear me or save me.*

Gerry burst into my room with a gun and pointed it at my head. I shut my eyes and started screaming and begging, "Please, don't shoot me! I promise I'll be good. I'll do anything you want."

"I warned you what would happen if you disobeyed me," he said.

"I'm sorry. I love you," I cried. "I promise I'll never disobey you again." I told him I wanted to have sex with him.

He put the gun down and got onto the bed. I didn't dare complain or resist. I hoped he would change his mind about killing me.

When he was done, he got up and said, "Get dressed. We're going for a ride."

As he was driving me toward the lake, I noticed a garbage bag between us on the seat of the truck. I began to shake, thinking that he planned to suffocate me.

It was the middle of the day and there was no one around. He told me to get out of the truck. I obeyed and began walking toward the lake with him. Suddenly, he pulled out a knife and plunged it into my chest. I saw blood everywhere. I just remember going into shock. I couldn't believe it was happening. I was totally petrified. I thought that was it. I can't describe the fear when you think you have no more time. Sure that I was dying, I prayed harder than I had ever prayed in my life, crying out to God to save me. Then I lost consciousness.

ESCAPE FROM GERRY

CHAPTER FOUR

AFTER I GOT OUT OF THE HOSPITAL, THINGS WENT ON AS USUAL. My mother never mentioned the stabbing to me. All she did was ask me if I was okay.

Shortly before my thirteenth birthday, I learned that Gerry was planning to be away for a few days. I was overjoyed. Not only was I going to be allowed to have a party, but I would have a few days free of Gerry! I invited a number of classmates from school. Much to my surprise, many said they would come. I was thrilled!

Three days before the scheduled party, Gerry was away. Mom asked me to sleep in her bedroom with her. I thought that was odd, but I'd learned that it didn't pay to ask questions.

The next morning, as I got ready for school, Mom told me that my brother Brian would be staying home with her. I went off to school obediently and without comment, but was puzzled by Mom's mysterious behaviour.

After lunch that afternoon, I looked up from my desk to see the principal walk into the classroom. I started trembling. Every time I saw the principal, bad things happened. He asked to see me in the hallway.

Once outside the classroom, the principal told me that my mother had called the school with instructions for me to get my brother and sister from the junior end and meet her in the parking lot, where she would be waiting in a taxi.

Now I was really confused. What on earth was going on?

I told my teacher and my friend who sat beside me in class that I would see them in a few days. Then I went to get Katy and Doug. When we got to the taxi where Mom was waiting, I couldn't stand the suspense any longer. I asked Mom what was happening.

"Not now. I'll explain later," she said. We took the taxi to the gas station, and got out. Then Mom told us that we were taking a bus to North Bay, and then another one to the hospital where we would visit Grandma.

"Is Grandma okay?" I asked, fearfully.

"Not now," Mom said again. "I'll explain once we're on the next bus."

I was more and more confused. Grandma had been in a semi-coma in Milton District Hospital for the past seven years. Mom had rarely spoken of her since the day she'd had her aneurysm. She had never taken us to visit her before. Of course I wanted to see Grandma again, but why now? Why the sudden urgency after all these years?

In North Bay, we boarded a bus that read "Toronto" on the front. After we had travelled a while, I asked Mom again what was going on.

Sitting beside me, she told me that she knew Gerry was having sex with me.

My whole body went numb. I hadn't seen this coming. Part of me couldn't believe what I had just heard.

She went on to say that she had overheard things in my bedroom one night. She asked me why I hadn't said anything. She asked me if her suspicions were true.

I was in shock and didn't answer. I didn't know what to say, but I didn't deny anything.

She said we were actually going to Toronto, not Milton, as she had told us. She said that we were leaving Gerry for good. She hadn't told me before because Mattawa was a small town and she was afraid I might let something slip that could get back to Gerry. She was scared he might come after us, trying to get custody of Ian, his only biological child. She didn't want Gerry to know where we were going. Then she asked if I would be willing to testify in court to the abuse if a custody battle ensued. I said that I would.

Having dropped her bombshell, my mom returned to her seat. I sat staring out the window, unseeing, trying to process her words. I had no idea what to do with the information I had just received.

My first emotion was anger. I was angry that I wasn't going to have my birthday party—my first one ever! People I had never expected to come had actually said yes to my invitation. I had been looking forward to it for weeks, and now, instead, we were on a bus to Toronto. I was angry that I never had a chance to say goodbye to my best friend, Nancy. I was angry that Mom had asked me why I hadn't said anything about the abuse. I had tried to, and it had almost cost me my life.

I was also scared—scared of moving to a big city like Toronto, scared of facing a new school and starting over, trying to make new friends, scared that Gerry might come looking for us.

Another part of me was relieved that I would never again have to be afraid of going to bed, listening for Gerry's footsteps. I was relieved that I no longer had to live in fear of him killing me.

All these emotions tumbled inside me during the six-hour ride. As we approached the city, my brothers and sister and I sat up excitedly, pointing at every building that was more than four stories tall, asking Mom if that was the CN Tower. We were in awe of the lights, the buildings, and the traffic. Mattawa was a small town with a population under five thousand. The tallest building there was three stories. We had never heard of McDonalds, Burger King, or Dairy Queen.

From the Dundas Street bus terminal, we took a taxi to a place called Family Residence. My excitement drained away as I realized this was a shelter for homeless people. It was crowded with kids and adults.

We shared one room as a family, and ate in a dining room with at least a hundred other people. One woman loved flashing all the children.

I'm sure that my mother hoped this would be a new beginning for us, a place where we could forget the past and put it all behind us. Maybe she had thought I would feel relieved and happy, but it wasn't that simple for me. All I felt was fear and hopelessness. I can't even express how alone I felt. I had learned from the past that no one wanted to hear about my feelings. There was no safe place for me to talk about all the pain and horror and confusion I carried inside. I couldn't just will it away or pretend that nothing had happened.

On Monday we started at the school across the street. When I walked into my classroom, I was startled to see that my teacher was Chinese, and many of my classmates were Portuguese. I had heard of China and Portugal before, but I had assumed that people there were white and spoke English or French, because that was all I had ever experienced.

We had gym the first day. After class, the teacher told me that I needed to take a shower. I was mortified. I didn't mind showering, but I was unused to open showers. I couldn't bring myself to get naked in front of my classmates. I was sure that everyone would be able to tell what Gerry had done with me as soon as they saw my body.

I sat on the bench in my clothes, waiting for the bell to ring. The teacher walked into the locker room and asked why I wasn't showering. I didn't know how to answer, so I said that I didn't want to. She said that showering after gym was mandatory, but no matter what she said, I couldn't bring myself to show my body. I refused. She started yelling at me in front of everyone. The bell rang and the Grade Eight students came in, but she kept yelling. I was humiliated. All I wanted was to disappear.

A week later, I was on my way to school after lunch at the hostel when a bald man drove slowly by me and yelled out his window, "How much do you charge?"

I didn't know what he was talking about. I approached his window and asked him what he meant. He ordered me to get in. Shocked at his tone, I swore at him and refused. He parked and got out of his car.

Scared, I ran as fast as I could, but he chased me. Quickly, I decided to run up Kensington Market, one of the busiest sections in Toronto. I managed to lose him in the crowd. Then I made my way back to the Family Residence. I was in a panic, and told my mom and the staff what had happened. They called the police, who questioned me and wrote out a report.

We lived in the hostel from April to July. My mother met Phil there, a single father of two sons. She found a house for us to rent, and Phil got an apartment for himself and his sons. Mom took us to visit him on weekends.

On one of these weekends, I woke up in the night to find Phil lying naked on the other side of the couch. He had been out drinking and wasn't aware I was there. It was an innocent mistake, but dynamite went off in my head.

It's going to happen again! I thought. I felt as though he was another Gerry, and he was going to hurt me or kill me. Terrified, I decided to prevent that from happening by burning us all to death.

A few weeks later, while everyone was asleep, I poured gasoline on some clothes in the bathroom and lit them on fire. I hid the gas can under Phil's son Christopher's bed, so the authorities would blame him. Christopher had accidentally caused a fire once before, so people would naturally think he had started this one.

After starting the fire, I went back to bed and lay awake. I'm not sure what would have happened if my brother hadn't got up to go to the bathroom. He ran back and told me, "There's a fire in the bathroom!" I pretended surprise and started waking everyone up. By that time, the place was full of thick smoke. My mom called the fire department and we all got out.

Both the fire department and the police questioned Christopher. Suspicion naturally fell on him. Although he protested his innocence, after the authorities left, my mother beat him in front of me. I had to watch, afraid that if I confessed, my mother would beat me.

As a result of this incident, Children's Aid took Phil's oldest son away. Tormented with guilt, I decided to commit suicide. I was fourteen.

While babysitting for a neighbour, I saw a bottle of pain medication in the bathroom cabinet. I knew I couldn't take the pills right then, because I was babysitting, so I put them in my pocket. The idea of taking an overdose haunted me. In the past I had wished many times that I was dead, but I had never actually thought about acting on those thoughts. Even at this point, I didn't really want to die, but I was hurting so badly inside and didn't know how to communicate it. I thought that maybe if I took some pills, people would become aware of what I was going through and help me. I was filled with anger and confusion about Gerry's abuse, but Mom had made it clear that it was taboo to talk about it. She wanted me to forget. I tried, but couldn't. I was screaming on the inside with rage and pain and longing for someone to help me.

I kept the pills under my pillow for two days. Then, after a fight with my mom, I ran upstairs to my room and dumped the pills out on my bed. I counted fifty-one of them. I chewed them one by one like Smarties.

I didn't really want to die at that moment; I was just mad and confused and didn't know how else to express it. As soon as I had swallowed the last of the little white pills, I phoned a friend to tell her. Her parents called my mom to tell her that I had overdosed.

My mother asked me if it was true and I said yes. She became furious and yelled at me. She called 911.

I was taken by ambulance to the hospital. Doctors and nurses were running all around me, doing tests, starting IVs, taking bloodwork. Then came the charcoal. I had to gag every mouthful of it while plugging my nose, but after three attempts I was successful.

Despite everything, I enjoyed all the unaccustomed attention. The nurses were compassionate and caring, although my mom sat beside me in silence, refusing to speak to me. I could sense her discomfort at my being in the spotlight.

I was asked repeatedly why I had taken the overdose. I wanted to answer them but was afraid to break the code of silence. My mother was staring at me, trying to intimidate me, and she succeeded. Talking about the past was against her rules. So I stayed silent.

Once the medical staff had stabilized me, I was transferred to the Hospital for Sick Children. Across the hall was a girl my age who was dying of leukaemia. Her name was Laura. She wore glasses and had a bald head from chemo. She would come to my bedside every day to play cards.

I really liked my new friend. I kept thinking, *Here she is, fighting for her life, surrounded by a loving family, and really wanting to see and live life. Yet here I am, not wanting to live, no family worth speaking of, and not caring what life holds in store.*

A few days later, my friend died. I couldn't help but cry for her. She was such a nice person, and she didn't deserve to have her life taken from her like that.

After two weeks, I was transferred to the psychiatric unit for another five weeks. My family would come once a week for family meetings. That included Mom, Phil, my siblings, and four-month-old Brittany, the newest addition to the family. I greeted them all, except for Brittany. I hated her for being one more person in the household to rob me of my mother's attention. I also hated the fact that she was named after my beloved grandmother.

The nurses noticed that I ignored Brittany. One nurse sat me down one day and told me that Brittany was just an innocent baby. She hadn't asked to be born, and she didn't deserve my treatment of her. The nurse said, "I guarantee that if you love Brittany, she will love you back. That's the wonderful thing about children. They have so much love to offer."

I held onto these words, realizing that it was wrong of me to treat my sister so badly. I decided that I would love her and be her guardian angel from that day on. I would do everything in my power to keep her safe and make sure she was cared for properly.

"A REBELLIOUS BAD TEENAGER"

CHAPTER FIVE

The hospital contacted the Children's Aid Society about my suicide attempt. They interviewed my mother, who said, "I don't know why my daughter did this. She's just a rebellious, bad teenager."

My behaviour supported my mom's claim. At the hospital I was constantly getting into trouble for picking fights with other patients and running away, only to be brought back by the police. I overdosed on several occasions. I had hysterical outbursts and had to be pinned to the floor by staff. I spent many days confined to my room.

The psychiatric unit was based on a level system. Level one meant room confinement in your pyjamas, with no visitors. Level two was basically the same, except that you were allowed to attend group meetings. Level three allowed access to the whole unit in your street clothes. Level four allowed you to leave the unit to go to the cafeteria, snack machines or gift shop. I never made it to level four during my five-week stay.

Mom was embarrassed that I was in a psychiatric unit, so she told everyone that I was in hospital for a blood disorder. My family attended meetings, but she didn't want people knowing our business, so she instructed the family to lie.

I had no visitors. My grandfather came once, but wasn't able to see me. I had attempted suicide a few days before, and was on level one. The nurse kindly delivered a nice fruit basket from him, and said that he would like to give me a call when it was permitted.

A few days later, I phoned Grandpa to thank him. He was confused, because Mom had told me that I had a blood disorder. When he'd gotten to the hospital, he found out that I was on the psychiatric unit. I told him that I had no idea why Mom had said what she did. Inside, I felt that I must be an embarrassment to her.

I told Grandpa the truth. He listened and said, "I really care for you! If there is anything at all that you need, please let me know."

As I ended the conversation, I felt reassured. Someone cared! I wished I could live with him, but I was afraid to ask. I didn't think I could bear it if he rejected me.

I wasn't the only person who thought it would be better for me to live somewhere else. People from Children's Aid came to see me while I was in the hospital and decided that because of the issues between me and Mom, I would be better off in a group home. However, there was no space available for me at the time, so they decided that I should go home until room was available. I thought that would take only a few weeks. I had no idea what a group home was, but I was sure it would be better than living with my mother.

A month went by with no word. I thought they had forgotten about me. I was desperate to go to a group home, but the only way I knew how to communicate my needs was to pop pills. After my first overdose, people had dropped everything to respond to me, so I did it again. Once again I was taken to emergency, stabilized, and transferred to the psychiatric ward. At that point, my mother willingly signed me over to the care of Children's Aid, and I was taken to the first of what would be many group homes.

I was a problem in the group homes just as I had been at the hospital. I refused to accept authority. My parents had abused their authority over me, and I wasn't going to submit to anyone again. As soon as I learned the rules in one place, I made a point of breaking them. I fought continually with the other residents, sassed the staff, skipped school, broke curfew, and attempted suicide. I often fantasized about running in front of a car and getting hit. I threw bleach in my eyes, swallowed cleaning fluids, and smashed my hands with bottles, trying to break my bones. I drank every day, and smoked dope whenever I got the chance.

I was aching for someone to love me, but so afraid of being victimized again that it was easier to pretend I hated the world and everyone in it than to let myself be vulnerable.

The thought of running away seemed more and more appealing. It scared me, but on the other hand, some of the other residents were chronic runners. How bad could it be? It had to be better than living with all these rules and regulations. Still, the idea of being alone on the streets terrified me. If I could convince someone to go with me, it wouldn't be as frightening.

I had a friend in the group home named Aimee. It wasn't hard to persuade her to run away with me. We figured that the four cheese sandwiches and fifty cents we had should last us a week before we had to worry about food. We pretended to head to school together but kept going, although we had no idea where.

We spent the whole day and most of the night walking, stopping periodically to eat one of our sandwiches or get a drink of water from a park fountain. Our appetites were bigger than we had expected. By suppertime we were out of food and money.

We weren't worried yet. We were sure that one of us should be able to get a job before starvation caught up with us. We passed many people during the night, but no one took notice of us. Apparently the sight of two young girls roaming the streets in the wee hours was not abnormal.

Eventually we were cold and exhausted. Aimee suggested we sleep in the stairwell of an apartment building she knew about a few blocks away. That sounded good to me. When we got there, I quickly dozed off, only to be awakened by the sound of footsteps from someone leaving their apartment. I woke Aimee, and we ran out of the building. As we ran, I saw a man standing in a window with a housecoat on, wide open. He was buck naked. I pointed it out to Aimee, and she started to laugh.

"Come on," she said. "I know this guy. We can get something to eat."

I was leery about the idea. On the other hand, I was starving.

Apart from being naked, the strange man seemed friendly. He offered us cookies, which I was happy to accept. He started flashing his naked body and encouraging us to go into his bedroom with him. I was getting extremely uncomfortable, but Aimee was laughing and acting as if she enjoyed the whole situation.

She turned to me. "Linda, it's up to you. I'll do whatever you want," she said.

I couldn't believe she was putting me in this spot. The last thing I wanted to do was have sex with this man, but I felt cornered.

"I'm okay with it if you are, but I would like to eat and freshen up first," I said.

The guy offered to go shopping for groceries, so he could cook us up a feast while we stayed in his apartment and freshened up. As soon as he left, I tried to talk to Aimee about how I was feeling, but she responded, "Don't worry, he's harmless. Just follow my lead."

I felt trapped. Being alone on the streets without Aimee was even more terrifying to contemplate than having sex with a stranger. I went into the bathroom to try to figure out a way to get out of this predicament. The only thing I could come up was popping pills. Taking an overdose had become a form of communication to me. It had worked in the past and would likely work now.

To my dismay, there were no pills in the medicine cabinet.

What kind of person lives without medication? I thought. *Doesn't everyone take pills of some sort? Now what?*

I kept searching for something to swallow. The only thing I could find was a can of deodorant. I decided to spray the contents into my mouth and swallow it. Then I used the phone in the bathroom to call an ambulance, pretending to be a friend reporting a suicide attempt. When I came out of the bathroom, I said nothing to Aimee about what I had done. The man returned with the groceries and began to make something to eat. Minutes later, both the police and the ambulance arrived.

There was a lot of commotion and panic at their arrival, but I was focused on escaping the apartment and getting safely into the waiting ambulance. As I was leaving, I heard the police questioning the man about his relationship with me, but all that mattered to me was getting away from that place.

The ambulance attendants asked me what I had taken. I told them I had consumed a can of deodorant. They struggled to keep straight faces as they took my vital signs. When they dropped me off at the hospital, they told me that I was the "nicest smelling person in Emergency." I'm sure I gave them the best laugh they'd had all night.

That adventure earned me a night in the hospital and a week of grounding at the group home. Still, my rebellion and self-destructive behaviour continued. In addition to that, I experienced night terrors that made me afraid to go to sleep. I often stayed up for days at a time. When I did sleep, I would start screaming and yelling in the middle of the night and become violent, often hurting anyone who tried to wake me. In the morning, I wouldn't remember much, other than a feeling of someone chasing me while I tried desperately to get away.

My mother came in frequently for family meetings. She always claimed to be the perfect mother of a rebellious daughter who hated authority. She was very convincing. It was easy to believe her, since staff also found me to be rebellious and attention-seeking. What nobody seemed to realize was how much I was suffering. I was communicating it in the only way I knew. I was drowning and lost inside and didn't know how to find my way out.

One time I was brought to the York Finch Hospital after another suicide attempt. While there, I confided in an occupational therapist that I had been abused by my stepfather and his brother-in-law. She did some role-playing with me to help me talk to my mom about it. When Mom came, and I did as the therapist had coached me to do, Mom stood up and said, "That's not true! That couldn't have happened. Why are you lying?" She was so furious that she pushed the bed into me and walked out.

I was constantly going from group home to group home. I was too young to be on my own, but few of the homes would put up with me for long. It got so that I didn't bother to unpack my few possessions when I moved to a new place. I kept my clothes and personal effects in a garbage bag, knowing that before long my new home would tire of me and give me the boot. But when I turned sixteen, the intake worker at my newest group home told me that I was running out of chances. At sixteen I could legally live on my own. She warned me that if I didn't turn my behaviour around and abide by the rules, I would find myself on the street with nowhere to go.

That scared me, and I decided to begin cooperating. I stopped skipping school and actually made the honour roll, which shocked me as much as it did everybody else. I also got a part-time job at McDonalds. I was very excited about that. It was my first real job other than babysitting or delivering newspapers.

Shortly after that, while walking to work and taking a shortcut through an alley between two stores, I was approached by a man. My heart began racing in panic, but I decided to act calm and continue walking. The next thing I knew, the man reached for me. Fear seared through my entire body. Reacting instinctively, I kicked him in the groin. He doubled over and I began running, faster than I ever had in my life before. Glancing over my shoulder, I saw him jump into a car and start driving toward me. I ran to a populated street and headed home.

When I arrived at the group home, I was breathless and shaking in fear. I told the staff what had happened. They called the police, who came to talk to me. They asked me to come to the station with them, where they escorted me into an interview room and questioned me for an hour. One of the officers told me that he didn't believe me. He said that I was a prostitute who had been fighting with my pimp. They threatened to charge me with obstructing justice, and told me how much I would love it in jail, where the lesbians would be all over me. They said they were going to put the word out on the street that I was nothing but a rat.

I was bewildered. I had no idea what a pimp was, or a prostitute. I didn't care if they put the word on the street, because I didn't live on the street and didn't know anyone who did. But my fear of jail, and of being abused or raped there, was very real. My stepfather had always said I would one day be locked up. Now his prediction seemed about to come true.

At that point, I stopped talking. I just wanted to go home where I was safe. That angered the officers even more. They interpreted my silence as an admission of guilt. They said that they were done with me for now, but they would be watching me.

They called the home to send someone for me. When the staff member arrived, they told her that I was a prostitute, and that they highly suspected I was involved with drugs as well.

When we got back, she took me to the office, where she told me what the police had said. She said that things were about to change. I would no longer be allowed to be alone with any of the other residents. All of my mail and phone calls would be screened. They didn't want me to lure the new girls into drugs or prostitution.

I felt perplexed and hurt. It seemed like I was in a nightmare and couldn't wake up. I had been at Arrabon House for eight months—much longer than I had lasted at any other group home. I had no friends outside the home, and was always home, except for school and work. My attendance could be verified at both places. How could I possibly be involved in prostitution or drugs? They had known me and seen my behaviour over the past eight months. How could they possibly believe the police over me? It just proved once again that I could never trust anyone in authority. I was truly on my own.

As I lay in bed that night, replaying the day's events over and over, I kept asking myself what had gone wrong. What had started out as a normal day had turned into a nightmare through no fault of mine. I thought about what the police had said to me, and how they had threatened me with jail. Then I thought about the new restrictions placed on me at Arrabon House, totally undeserved. The more I thought about it, the angrier I felt.

There was no way I could continue to live in this home. I had always struggled with trusting people. Now, what little trust I had built over the past eight months was destroyed.

In the middle of the night, while everyone else was asleep, I got up, packed a knapsack of clothes, and slipped away into the night. I had no idea where I was going. All I knew was that sleeping on a park bench, or huddled on a heating vent somewhere, seemed preferable to jail, or living in a place where I wasn't trusted or believed.

DR.
ARMSTRONG

CHAPTER SIX

I SPENT THE NIGHT ROAMING THE STREETS, WITH NO PLAN. AFTER several hours, I found a phone booth and searched through the phonebook in hopes of finding a street hostel. I came across a place called Stop 86 and went there, planning to spend a few days.

A few nights later, I had one of my night terrors. Another resident tried to wake me, and I punched her in my sleep. The hostel told me I had to leave. Despondent, I decided to hang myself. I shut myself into the closet in my room and began to hook up a belt on a coat hanger, when staff members walked in on me. They called a crisis centre to come and get me.

It was that night, at the crisis centre, that I met Dr. Harvey Armstrong for the first time. When I walked into his office, I stood in the corner, staring at the floor. He began asking me questions. Shock went through me as I heard him say, "Have you ever been sexually abused?"

I stood, frozen in disbelief. Up until that point I had always been labelled rebellious, angry, and having a problem with authority. Nobody ever suspected the hurt and pain that was behind my behaviour. Until now.

I didn't know how to respond. My body was filled with terror. I refused to look at him. I don't know why I was so afraid, but he seemed to understand. He assured me that everything would be okay. He assured me that things would get better in my life if I hung in there and agreed to see him on a regular basis.

"No pressure," he said, "but my desire for you is that someday you'll be healthy enough that you'll be willing to pursue justice. When that day comes, I promise you that I'll be right with you all the way to walk you through the process. I'll attend the hearings, I'll take you there, I'll be there."

He said that the first priority was to find me shelter, and he prescribed medication to help with the night terrors.

I was taken to a youth hostel called Under 21. Within days, I was introduced to the world of drugs and prostitution. Under 21 was in the centre of the red light district, across from Allen Gardens, one of Toronto's most notorious parks. The park was full of drug activity and was referred to as Hookerville. I couldn't even walk to the store without passing a prostitute, or having a driver go by asking me how much I charged. Most of the residents at Under 21 were drug addicts, prostitutes, and pimps.

I found myself mesmerized by and drawn to this dark world, although I didn't know why. Maybe it was because I was forbidden by the hostel staff to go near Allen Gardens, coupled with the fact that I had already been accused of being a prostitute and drug-dealer by the police. Maybe it was the sense of acceptance and family I felt from the other residents at Under 21. Whatever the reason, I quickly became what I had already been labelled by others.

I was too shy to dress up and stand on street corners like the other prostitutes, so I would cross the street to the park, wearing my regular jeans and t-shirts. I would sit on a park bench, knowing that a customer would approach me before long. Within minutes I would have a client.

The idea that I could be putting myself in danger didn't cross my mind. Abuse had been so much a part of my life that I couldn't fathom anything happening that was worse than I had already experienced. I felt so dead and worthless inside that it didn't seem to matter. I had come to believe that I was dirty and useless. I felt so unloved and uncared for that I couldn't think clearly or make healthy choices. I thought I didn't deserve to be happy. Having a life outside the one I knew seemed impossible.

Prostituting myself was a matter of dissociating and separating my mind from my body so that I was out of touch with where I was and what was happening. Initially I didn't care about the money. I was satisfied if the customer bought me a hamburger afterward.

Sometimes the men would get rough, and I would resist. That led to being raped. I learned that, just as with Gerry, it was safer to cooperate.

Once I began with drugs, I started charging for my services. I needed the money to support my addiction.

The streets were a scary place. I felt vulnerable and trusted no one. I even had to tie my shoelaces around my ankles to prevent people from stealing them. I was frequently raped, but that was just part of my life, the only life I knew. Each time it happened I accepted it as being what I deserved.

My best friend on the street was Tara. Her family lived in Vancouver and she had run away from home when she was twelve because her father was sexually abusing her. She had hitchhiked to Toronto where she'd been on the streets for five years. She showed me the ropes: where to get food and shelter, and how to survive. She often shared her heating vent with me in the winter, and she helped me build a lean-to shelter along Black Creek Drive, right behind where my family lived. I sometimes slept there in a sleeping bag in sub-zero weather.

A year later, Tara accidentally overdosed and died. She didn't have a funeral. It was as though her family didn't care, and she just vanished from the world.

After her death, the world was a very lonely place. We had been close and spent a lot of time together. Now she wasn't here and I was alone in the world again, having to fend for myself. I continued to sleep on her heating vent or in my lean-to, but sometimes the cold was too much and I was forced to take shelter.

Sometimes I broke down and phoned Dr. Armstrong, and he would come and rescue me from the elements. Calling him was very hard for me. He often told me that he would help in any way he could, but I struggled with asking. I was very afraid of rejection. I also believed that I didn't deserve his concern. I was a nobody, not worth anyone taking the time and effort to help.

I couldn't explain this to Dr. Armstrong, but I did like him and felt that he cared. If my asking were to scare him into rejecting me, I was sure it would destroy me inside. He knew that if I asked for help, I was truly desperate. If I asked for food, it was because I hadn't eaten for three days. If I asked for a place to stay, it was because my fingers were so frozen that I could no longer feel them. Dr. Armstrong helped every time I asked, but my fear of rejection was so strong that I couldn't shake it.

Since it was often in the middle of the night when I called, he would bring me back to his home and let me stay in the guest room. His wife wrote about those times in her book, *Confessions of a Trauma Therapist*:

> *Linda was as guarded and anti-social as E. was charming and fun. Linda tended to hide in her bedroom, our guest room. She was a homely girl, ill at ease in her heavy body and not interested in makeup or attractive clothing. She suffered from dissociative identity disorder, which meant she had what's called an alter—a split-off part of the personality that functions independently of the affected individual. Linda's alter existed for sex. This other part of her was outrageously sexual with Harvey. I would enter his study to see her looking seductively at him, trying to persuade him to succumb to her charms. He, for his part, would just continue at his desk, doing what he was doing in an attempt to assure the alter there was no chance of anything happening.*[1]

I have no memory of the incidents Mrs. Armstrong writes about, but I do remember testing his boundaries at times during scheduled appointments in his office, trying to find out if he could be trusted or if he would abuse me as other men had. This went on for several years. I would flirt and make suggestive comments. He would always respond the same way: "Linda, I think you're very beautiful, but I'm your doctor and I'm not willing to cross any boundaries with you." He passed every test I gave him.

---

1 Mary K. Armstrong, *Confessions of a Trauma Therapist* (New York, NY: BPS Books, 2010), 94.

From time to time I would tire of the streets and decide to give another group home a chance, but always with the same results. Before long I would be kicked out and end up back on the street.

The other person I stayed in touch with was my grandfather. I often phoned him. He would come into the city from Burlington to take me out for lunch and shopping for clothes and whatever I needed. I felt very close to Grandpa. I felt that he really cared for me and was there if I needed anything. Although he always said, "Just ask if you need anything," I never did. I was afraid that he, too, would reject me. The thought of that was unbearable. I loved Grandpa and couldn't picture him not being in my life.

I also kept in contact with my family, but never mentioned my way of life or addiction. I was sure my mother would never understand. Sometimes I talked her into letting me come home, but I never stayed long. I hated it there. The only reason I ever came was to see my little sister Brittany. I had become very attached to her, and it was important to me to stay connected and look out for her.

When Brittany was nine or ten, I looked at her and realized, "Man, that's how old I was when I was abused!" She was just an innocent, defenceless child. I thought I would kill anyone who ever tried to harm her.

Things had deteriorated at home, unless they had always been that way and I never noticed. My mother's personal hygiene and housekeeping were nonexistent. Floors were rarely washed or vacuumed. Both bathrooms were filthy. One was clogged, and my mother left it that way, making no effort to fix it. The ceiling in the other was falling down, and always leaked. Dirty dishes were rinsed under running water, not washed with soap. The basement was filled with dog urine and faeces.

My mother was living in Ontario Housing at the time. I often asked her why she didn't call them to fix the toilet and ceiling in the bathrooms. She would say, "Why bother, since they'll just break down again?" I think she was afraid that if the authorities saw the state of the house, she would be evicted.

My siblings were always dirty and unkempt. There was rarely any food at home besides bread and peanut butter. I was severely allergic to peanuts.

I didn't remember things being this bad when I was a child. At that time, my mother had cooked and baked, and on Sundays we usually had roast, spaghetti, or stew.

The worst part about coming home was the cockroaches. My family's home was totally infested. There were millions of roaches running around. Everywhere you looked, you could see them on the walls. If I slept over, I didn't dare walk into the kitchen in the middle of the night for a glass of water. The one time I did, I turned on the light and saw zillions of them all over the floor and counter. I couldn't step anywhere or touch the counter without touching one. After that experience, I stayed in bed all night, wrapped in my blankets, terrified that a cockroach would crawl into my mouth while I was asleep.

Roaches were in the fridge, cupboards, saltshakers—even the furniture. I couldn't bring myself to eat or drink at home. I was afraid of accidentally swallowing a cockroach. If I was thirsty, I would cup my hands under the tap and drink that way, or bring cans of pop home with me. I didn't want to use the dishes at home because of the roaches. It was risky even to set my can of pop down, in case a roach fell in; so I would drink the whole can at once.

During these visits home, I would eat in restaurants, or go to the corner store for packaged munchies. If it was a special occasion, such as Christmas dinner, I boiled my plate and utensils beforehand, never added seasonings, and examined everything closely before putting it in my mouth.

When I went home, I made sure to bathe Brittany and take her out with me to eat. I often bought groceries for my brothers and sisters.

Brittany and I were very close. She would cry when I left. When I wasn't at home, I thought about her all the time and would call to make sure she was okay. I was concerned for her welfare and told Dr. Armstrong, who called Children's Aid. They phoned my mother to let her know they were coming, which gave her enough time to tidy the place up and make sure the kids were properly clean and dressed. So nothing changed.

I was continuing to see Dr. Armstrong every week during this period so I could get Valium from him to help with the night terrors. He was the staff psychiatrist at Youthdale Treatment Centre, which ran half a dozen different treatment group homes. He encouraged me to apply, to help get me off the streets. The very word "treatment" frightened me, but I really liked Dr. Armstrong, so I agreed to apply.

At my intake interview, it was decided that I would be best suited for their Aftercare program, designed for young people who were already quite independent. The goal of Aftercare was to help prepare us for living on our own, without addiction and unsafe choices. Because my history of being kicked out of group homes was related to my problems with authority and rules, Aftercare seemed a good fit for me. I would have much more independence and fewer rules to follow. I agreed to give it a try.

I was seventeen when I moved in a week later. I placed my garbage bag with few belongings under the bed. I decided not to bother unpacking, since I was sure this experience would end the same way all the others had.

To my surprise, there was only one other resident when I moved in. To me, this was paradise! Lynn was out working or socializing most of the time, so I usually had the staff's undivided attention. I was unused to getting so much attention, and I loved it. I would spend hours sitting and talking with staff.

Rules were lax. This was a new experience for me, and I enjoyed it. There was no structured program other than having to work and/or attend school. Curfew was 1:00 a.m. We were expected to share in the cooking and shopping duties, in order to prepare us for when we moved out on our own. But this was no big deal for me.

The best part of living there was the sense of independence and responsibility it gave me. At first I bucked some of the rules, such as looking for a job or not staying out all night. I was never disciplined for my actions. The staff would speak with me and encourage me to make more responsible decisions.

Shortly after moving in, I got into an argument with a staff member. I can't remember what it was about, so it was probably something minor. What I do remember vividly was how angry I became. I stormed out of the house, slamming the door behind me, causing its stained-glass panel to shatter. When I saw the broken glass, I panicked and began running up the street, sure that I was in big trouble.

At the end of the street I stopped, not sure what to do. I started crying, sorry for my actions. Aftercare was so different from all the other places. The staff was kind and seemed to really care about me. I would never have admitted it to them, but I actually liked it there. Now I was going to be kicked out once again. I was afraid to go back. I couldn't handle their rejection. So I decided to head downtown.

As I walked, I told myself that the streets weren't all that bad. Maybe I could check out Under 21 and see if I could get a bed there. The more I thought about it, the more I wished I could turn the clock back and undo the slammed door. I really wanted to keep living at the Aftercare home. Finally I decided to take my chances and go back and apologize. Maybe they would give me a second chance.

When I got back, I saw a black bag taped to the broken window. So I really had done it. I hadn't dreamed it.

I walked inside and the staff member was there waiting. The first thing she said was, "I'm glad you came back. I was so worried about you."

"I'm sorry," I said.

"It's okay. The important thing is that you're home and safe. You need to know what was going on inside of you to cause that much rage, but it's late now. How about getting a good night's sleep, and we'll talk more tomorrow? We have a staff meeting in the morning, so we will discuss the incident as a staff team to decide if there should be a consequence, and if so, what it should be."

As I lay in bed, I kept replaying the night's events over in my mind. I couldn't believe the reaction of the staff member. I wasn't used to people being that nice to me, especially after I had damaged property. I was bothered by the idea of getting a consequence. Couldn't they just accept my apology and forget about the broken window? Eventually the evening's shadowy images faded and I drifted off to sleep.

The next morning, I went to school. The end of the day couldn't come quickly enough. I wanted to get home and face the music for my behaviour the previous night. The suspense was unbearable.

When I got home, the program's director met me at the door. *Here it goes*, I thought. *I'm in for it now.*

She sat me down and said that the staff had decided I should pay for the window myself. I couldn't believe my luck. No grounding, extra chores, or being kicked out. I already had some money saved from a summer job.

"The window will cost $250 to replace," she continued. "You are not allowed to pay for it out of your bank account."

She told me I had six months to find a part-time job and pay for the window, or the staff would renegotiate my consequence. She then asked me to sign a contract to make the agreement official.

I truly did learn my lesson. From then on, whenever I became angry with a staff member, I would start my usual yelling, screaming and storming around, but when I came to a door, I would stop long enough to shut it gently.

I began looking for part-time work, and was very excited when I quickly landed a job at Burger King. I had babysat, delivered newspapers, and worked a bit the previous summer at the Canadian National Exhibition, but now I had a regular paycheque! I asked for as many shifts as I could get, and was always ready to pick up shifts from people who needed to get out of theirs. I paid off the window in three months, and then had lots of money at my disposal. I saved some, and spent the rest on drugs and alcohol. Despite that, and the thirty hours a week I worked at Burger King, I maintained an A average in school. I was in Grade Twelve at the time.

I enjoyed my job and made a lot of friends. One night, close to closing time, my two managers told me they were going to stay after hours with some of the other workers and drink. They invited me to join them. Drinking was nothing new to me, so I was happy to stay with them and party.

I was used to drinking beer, but not hard liquor. I didn't want to lose my "cool" status by letting on, so I downed two large cups in quick succession. The room started spinning and I felt nauseous. I became drunker than I had experienced in my life, but was too stubborn to admit it. I was afraid they wouldn't want to hang out with a "rookie."

After a while, they decided we should go to a late-night restaurant. I desperately wanted to go home and sleep off the booze, but I didn't think I could make it back on my own. At the restaurant, I put my head down on the table, oblivious to everything around me. For a long time I just stared at my hand. I thought about trying to move it, but that felt like too much work. I concentrated on one finger, thinking that if I stared long enough I could will it to move.

At this point, the others realized that I'd had more to drink than I could handle, and decided that one of them should take me home by taxi. I vaguely heard someone asking for my address, but I had no idea where I lived. Then I felt someone going through my pockets, searching for information.

My escort got me home, carried me up the steps, and let us in with the keys she found in my pocket. The staff member was sleeping upstairs, so she left me on the couch and disappeared.

Early the next morning, I woke up with a dreamlike memory of the previous night. I hurried up to my room before anyone else was up. To my relief, the incident was never mentioned, so I got away with it that time.

Occasionally I got pot from friends at work. I didn't dare smoke it in the house, knowing I would have been kicked out for sure. I usually went to the park around the corner to smoke it. No matter how discreet I thought I was being, the staff could always tell by my behaviour and the odour on my clothes. They often talked to me about it, expressing their concern. I would promise not to do it again, but I had no intention of keeping those promises. I just wanted them off my back.

Inside, I was depressed, confused, hurt, and very alone. I didn't know how to communicate how I felt. All I knew was that whenever I had tried in the past, I had been rejected and disbelieved. I was convinced that what lay inside me was more powerful than I was. I was terrified of myself. Drugs and alcohol gave me a way to escape all these feelings for a while.

Outside work and school, I had no life. Apart from contact with the odd ex-resident of a previous group home, I had no friends. I was no longer teased at school, but still felt like the odd man out. At lunchtime, people went off with their group of friends, and I sat alone in the cafeteria. I began going for walks at lunch so it wouldn't be obvious how alone I was.

FAMILY

CHAPTER SEVEN

During my stay at Youthdale, my grandfather called and invited me to go with him to London, Ontario to visit my aunt and uncle. Excited at the thought of seeing my relatives again, I arranged with him to pick me up on Halloween. We stopped at a restaurant for supper and then headed off.

After driving a while, Grandpa said, "It's getting late and I'm tired. How about we get a motel room for the night and leave first thing in the morning? That way we'll arrive during the daylight."

We checked into a motel and I sprawled on the bed, turning on the TV and flipping through channels. Grandpa stretched out beside me, which felt weird, but there was only one bed in the room. I dismissed my discomfort about the situation. He was my grandfather, after all.

As I was clicking through channels with the remote, my grandfather suddenly leaned over and tried to kiss me on the lips. Trembling in shock, I pushed him away, jumped up, and reached for my jacket. I couldn't believe what had just happened. He was my grandfather! Grandpas weren't supposed to kiss granddaughters in that way.

My world started to crumble around me. I loved my grandpa and trusted him. How could he do it? He was the one person who had always been there for me. I'd thought he really cared!

As I grabbed for my things, Grandpa begged me not to leave. "I'm sorry," he said. "I promise to sleep on the floor if you'll stay."

Everything had happened so fast. I didn't know what to do. Finally, I decided to stay for the time being—as long as he stayed on the floor.

He quickly fell asleep, but I lay tossing and turning, replaying what had happened over and over. I still couldn't believe it. How could he? I hated him! He could have a heart attack and die as far as I was concerned.

From that moment on, I realized there was no one in my life I could trust.

The longer I listened to his heavy breathing, the more I loathed him. I decided I couldn't stand being in the same room with him. As he lay on the floor, I tiptoed out and hitchhiked back to Toronto.

When I got back, I decided not to say anything. I wanted to put the incident behind me, vowing never to see or speak to my grandfather again.

While I was at Youthdale, I continued to visit my family, mostly to see Brittany. It was important to me to stay connected with her and make sure she was being cared for properly. If she needed anything, I would get it for her. I loved to spoil her and make her happy.

My mother was a whole other story. We rarely got along. Inside, I blamed her for not protecting me as a child. I blamed her for not being there for me. I tried many times to talk to her about the abuse and what was going on inside me, but she would lash out and blame me, even denying that the abuse had happened. She called me a liar and said that I had made the abuse up!

This made me furious. How could she not believe me? She had to have known! How could she not? What had she thought Gerry had been doing in my room at night? Why had she thought Gerry had been taking me out for drives? What had gone through her mind when she'd found Katy sleeping on the couch in the living room? She had told me on the bus to Toronto that she'd known, so why was she now denying it?

I ached to hear my mother say "I love you" and "I'm sorry." But those words would never come out of her mouth.

I began to believe that I was unloved and uncared for. If Mom had loved me, she would have been there for me. My hurt and loneliness festered into bitterness and hate toward my mom.

On the other hand, I desperately yearned for her love. I thought I had failed her somehow. Maybe, if I tried a bit harder, she would love me.

She never had much money, so whenever I went home I would buy groceries, take the family out to a restaurant, or buy that much-needed sofa or microwave. I fantasized about winning the lottery so that I could take my mom on her dream vacation to Australia or buy her a house.

When I bought things, she would be initially grateful, but it was always short-lived and we would soon resort to fighting again. I did love her, but the deep pain of her rejection made it impossible for me to overcome my resentment and anger.

Dr. Armstrong would get frustrated with me because I would spend all my money on buying things for Mom. I was trying to buy her approval. Eventually I realized that it wouldn't change the person she was.

I was always eager to see Mom and talk to her on the phone, but she inevitably pushed my buttons, causing me to explode. Every contact left me depressed, driving me to take pills or injure myself in some way. The staff at Aftercare and past group homes learned to dread me contacting my family. Some of the group homes banned me from making contact, knowing that the aftereffects would be bad.

I did make a few half-hearted suicide attempts while at Aftercare. I call them half-hearted because I had no intention of dying. I had perfected the art of attempted suicide. I knew exactly how many pills to take, and how long to wait before getting treatment so the attempts wouldn't be fatal. I always took the overdoses when people were around, and I always made sure someone knew and would get me to the hospital in what I called the safe time zone.

Once the hospital cleared me, I would be taken to the Youthdale Crisis Centre, where I got to see Dr. Armstrong. I was always happy to see him, not only because he seemed to really care, but, more importantly, because he seemed to understand. Not that I could let on that I liked him. I had been hurt and betrayed so many times before that I had built a wall around me a mile thick. I wasn't willing to let anyone through, not even Dr. Armstrong. However, after a few admissions and conversations with him, I agreed to see him on a regular basis.

After a year and a half at Youthdale, I decided to move out with my best friend Anne. As my discharge date approached, I got scared. For the first time in my life I was feeling stable and secure. I had also become attached to some of the staff and residents. Leaving was too frightening, so I decided to take another overdose. I hoped that an apparent suicide attempt would convince the staff at Youthdale to delay my discharge.

It didn't work this time. The supervisor came to the hospital to visit me and said, "I think your self-destructive behaviour is a result of your apprehensions about leaving in two weeks. We as a staff team feel that you are ready, and we do not think it would be beneficial to you to extend your discharge date."

I couldn't believe it. I was really angry. Things weren't supposed to turn out this way. I was so used to getting what I wanted after these episodes. For the first time, the supervisor was telling me I wasn't going to win, and they weren't going to give in.

I decided not to argue, because I knew she was right. After being discharged from the hospital, I went home for a week to prepare for my new life. My plan was to move in with Anne, who was living with her mother, while we looked for an apartment. Anne's mother was an alcoholic who was always at home, but she kept to herself. I was working at Burger King most of the time, but otherwise hibernated in the bedroom.

Anne and I quickly found a one-bedroom apartment in the back of a house, and moved in.

We wasted no time testing our newfound freedom. We quickly adapted to the partying lifestyle. I would work during the day, and crack open a beer as soon as I got home. On weekends, we did the bar scene.

The honeymoon stage lasted only two months. Anne and I began arguing constantly until we decided to part ways. I was very hurt by the loss of our friendship, but I was too proud to apologize or make amends. I had no idea where I would go. My job at Burger King didn't pay enough to support me.

I ended up sleeping on a cot in the manager's office in the basement of the Burger King where I worked. It wasn't a great option, but it was better than the streets or a hostel. I hated hostels, and found sleeping outside on a heating vent or park bench preferable. Hostels were overcrowded; they meant sleeping on a mat with a dozen other people who were all snoring and talking in their sleep. Those places always stank, too, since hygiene was a challenge for the homeless. I was also uncomfortable being around the mentally ill and addicts who were abundant in hostels. I knew that I had my own share of issues, but I hated who I was and found it hard living with people who had similar struggles.

During that time, I decided to visit my aunts and uncles in Nova Scotia with my sister Katy. We stayed with Aunt Lois and Uncle Bill.

My Aunt Jan worked for the answering service there, so she had everyone's contact information. I was unaware that my father—my real father, the one my mother had said was in jail—was living right there in the country outside Halifax. Unbeknownst to me, Aunt Jan contacted him to let him know I was in town.

The first I found out about it was when my grandmother—my dad's mother—phoned me at Aunt Lois' to invite me to dinner at her place to meet her and Dad.

I was beyond excited, but nervous and anxious as well. My grandmother was a tall, obese lady who pinched my cheeks as though I was a little kid and exclaimed, "Oh, we missed you so much! We're so happy to see you." In contrast, my grandfather was a skinny man, but quite friendly as well.

Dad was tall, with a beer belly, short black hair, and a glass eye from a childhood accident. I realized that I resembled him more than I did my mother. We gave each other a big bear hug.

Grandma had put out the red carpet in my honour: a roast beef dinner with mashed potatoes and all the trimmings. Dad's two young daughters from his second marriage were there as well: Mandy and Amber. I felt very shy, but welcome.

Grandma got out the family photo albums after dinner and showed me pictures of relatives I had never met or known about.

At the end of the evening, Dad said, "Oh, you've got to come to my place." Unfortunately, Katy and I were flying back to Toronto the next day.

Even though I said little all evening, I left feeling very connected with my newly discovered family. But I was angrier than ever at my mother. She had cut all of his pictures out of the photo album, and told me he was a drug addict and in prison. None of it was true.

Five months after that first visit, Dad sent plane tickets for me and Brian to visit him again. Brian was very excited. This time we stayed at

Dad's country home. We took care of the cows and chickens, which was great fun for us city kids. Dad's wife Beatrice was friendly, although not as warm and huggy as Dad. We stayed there for a couple of weeks, really getting to know him. He took us shopping and showed us around the country. I got comfortable very quickly.

Dad was very apologetic for abandoning us years ago. He explained that he had visited for a while after he and Mom had separated, but that stopped once she moved away. He knew Mom had left us in our grandmother's care. He had known Grandma, and known she would love us and take good care of us. He had lost touch by the time she became ill, so he knew nothing of what followed. I told him about our life with Gerry, and Dad seemed really distressed and sorry about it all.

Now that we were reacquainted with our father, Brian and I continued to visit him once or twice a year. Dad was a housing contractor, which meant that during the winter months he was on EI. Although none of what my mother said about him being in jail or a drug addict was true, he did have a drinking problem. It wasn't like Gerry's, who drank almost all the time and became violent. Dad didn't drink all week until Friday night, when he went out to the bar and drank until he passed out. Beatrice would come and get him, he would sober up, and then stay sober all week until the next Friday night, when the cycle would continue.

I told Dad about Gerry's abuse and my problems at home, but I didn't tell him about my lifestyle or my addiction issues. He didn't know anything about my living on the streets or my present situation sleeping in the basement of Burger King.

I became so depressed sleeping at Burger King that I overdosed again. I didn't want to die, but I didn't know any other way to communicate my pain. I was alone in the world and hated my existence. I was lost in bitterness, pain, and confusion and couldn't find my way back.

It wasn't that nobody had tried to help. Over the years I had met many doctors, nurses, and social workers who had done their best for me. But if I didn't know what was going on with me and why I was acting out in such a self-destructive way, how could they help? I didn't even know how to let them help me.

My suicide attempts no longer got me the attention I used to enjoy. I had become too well-known by all the hospitals in Toronto. The hospital staff had given up on me. No one asked anymore why I did what I did. It wasn't uncommon for a doctor to threaten to discharge me even while my blood levels were still toxic from the overdose, or for the staff to automatically put me in restraints. I had such a reputation that I was labelled a troublemaker.

It was obvious to me that the medical personnel had given up on me. They were frustrated with having to spend time on me when there were other patients who responded to treatment. I was no longer a vulnerable fourteen-year-old who elicited their compassion; I was a twenty-year-old chronic pill-popper who was beyond help, in their eyes.

Despite that, I still chose to take pills. I had no idea what I was trying to accomplish. I was so detached from my feelings that I didn't know why I did the things I did.

It might have been because my family was moving to Nova Scotia. At first I wanted to go with them, because I didn't want to be separated from Brittany. Also, my family still provided some kind of security blanket for me, even if it was a thin one. I knew I could go there to crash whenever I needed a place to sleep.

Still, I had survived this long on my own, and I would continue to survive.

WRESTLING WITH GOD

CHAPTER EIGHT

AFTER RECOVERING FROM THE OVERDOSE, I MET WITH THE HOSPITAL social worker and agreed to give another group home a shot. It was Ingles House, an Anglican group home, funded by a church. We were required to participate in Bible studies and prayers after meals. There was no TV, and we were expected to attend a church service every second Sunday. It sounded odd to me, but it couldn't be any worse than living on the streets.

I went through the motions at devotions and prayer time, but it was just an act to keep the staff off my back. Inside, I had no desire to know who God was. I had so much anger at God, who I blamed for the way my life had turned out. Beneath the anger was much pain and fear. I felt hurt and blamed God for taking my grandma away when I was six. I held Him responsible for all the abuse I had endured. I believed that He didn't care about me, and couldn't possibly love me. How could a loving God allow such atrocities to happen to me?

Deep inside I knew there was a God, and yearned to know Him, but I was so bitter that I rejected Him and pushed Him away even as I longed for Him. I believed that it was easier to reject Him than to risk Him rejecting me. Sometimes I even prayed to Satan, just to make God mad.

I told the people in the home that I had my own church so I wouldn't have to attend with them. On Sunday mornings, while they were at church, I would sit on a park bench freezing, preferring that to going into a house of God. I was so angry at God that I wanted nothing to do with Him. I was having a battle of wills with Him, conducting a one-way conversation. "You weren't there for me as a child, and You're not getting Your way now! I hate You and I'll stay out here and freeze before I go inside a church."

I kept this up for two years. I gave the best performance of my life at that house. To all appearances I was a "super Christian" who read her Bible and faithfully attended church. I rattled off Scriptures and declared my love for God, telling the other residents how I had accepted God back in the third grade. I even went so far as to be publicly baptized. I was held up as a spiritual role model to the other residents, when in reality I was a huge manipulator and deceiver.

Despite my blatant hypocrisy, I became very close to the staff and residents. This home wasn't like any of the other group homes I had been. Even though the rules were much stricter than anywhere else, the staff seemed to genuinely care about me. They always took time to talk with me, express fondness for me, and praise me for the example I set. I kept up the act because I enjoyed the way everyone seemed to look up to me.

That fall, back at Ingles House I began taking a two-year legal office administration course at college. I was still working at Burger King, working fifty hours a week. I found it hard to say no, so I was constantly working.

The staff at Ingles House was glad that I worked so much, because they dreaded my days off. When I was busy, I had no time to think about anything, but when I had a day off I would become depressed and have suicidal fantasies. I never acted on those thoughts, because it would have blown my super spiritual cover. Still, the staff was uncomfortable with my fantasies because they knew about my history of attempts.

Ingles House had a two-year limit on residency. They extended it for me to two and a half years so I could complete my legal administration course. It helped pass the time and give me something else to focus on. I maintained an A average and was a half semester away from earning my diploma when I started thinking, *What's the point?* I decided to withdraw from the course. The people at the registrar's office begged me not to drop out. The secretary said, "I'm confused as to why you want to withdraw. You're on the Dean's list. With your 3.59 GPA, you can skip the rest of the year and your finals and still graduate."

It didn't matter to me. My mind was made up. I believed that I would die soon. I was still very suicidal. I figured that since I wouldn't be around much longer, I wouldn't need that diploma. Why waste my time, or cut the rest of the year and suffer the embarrassment of dropping off the Dean's list?

In reality, I was terrified of failure and disappointment. My hopes had been crushed so many times that it seemed less painful to take control by sabotaging anything good in my life before anyone else could.

When I turned twenty-two, I had to leave. This was very hard for me. I had become attached to people there, which was a new experience for me. After leaving, I stayed in close contact with staff and residents who had become friends. Especially Lisa, a girl I had grown close to. We often got together for lunch or coffee. She seemed very spiritual, but at the same time confusing. She never spoke about her past, and I knew very little about her. But she was an all-round nice person who loved to laugh. I envied that, because I had difficulty laughing.

Then, one day, she jumped in front of a subway train. She didn't die, but she lost her arm. I was shocked. She had always seemed so together. I had no idea she was suicidal.

After losing her arm, Lisa ended up in a psychiatric hospital. I was angry and blamed her. I refused to visit her at first. I thought she was depressed over losing her arm, and felt that was her own fault. When I shared my feelings with the director of Ingles House, she told me that Lisa had schizophrenia, and heard voices in her head that had caused her to jump.

I didn't really understand, but I did realize then that Lisa was sick and hadn't caused her own predicament deliberately. She didn't have many friends. I knew that the right thing was to be there for her, so I went to visit.

I was uncomfortable in the hospital. All the walls were white. In the dining room, the residents ate from hospital trays; the doors were locked. People walked around like zombies. Of course, I had been a patient of several psychiatric units, but those units were always part of a general hospital rather than a psychiatric institution. The hardest part for me was coming in as a visitor. Up until now, I had always been the patient.

From Ingles House I moved into an apartment with a friend, Diane. Immediately she and I struggled, and I became very depressed. Diane was rarely home. She worked full-time and had an active social life. I often found myself home alone in the apartment. I wasn't used to that. I had spent most of my life on the streets, in hostels, or in group homes. I was the eldest child of six. As alone as I had felt in those circumstances, there had always been people around.

When I was alone, I had time to think about my childhood and family. Besides those painful thoughts, I hated being alone. I despised myself. I saw myself as a big failure, incapable of amounting to anything. I hated the person under my skin. It was becoming increasingly difficult to be alone with the person I despised more than anything else in the world.

After dropping out of school, I moved out of the apartment and began again bouncing from place to place. Depressed, I overdosed a few times, but the hospitals were used to me. They would stabilize me medically, then discharge me with nowhere to go. I hated this lifestyle, but I felt trapped and lost and didn't know how to get out.

Besides being homeless, I was out of school and unemployed. I had let go of my job at Burger King to focus on my college studies. I looked for work in a law office even though I had dropped out of my legal course. To my amazement, I was able to get a good position with The Law Society of Upper Canada.

I could hardly believe my luck. Up until that time, the only work I had done had been in fast food, babysitting, and delivering newspapers. This was a dream come true. I had a real job that allowed me to live quite comfortably! Initially I felt uncomfortable working in an office with auditors and lawyers, but it didn't take me long to fit in and make friends with people.

The benefits and regular socials were more than I had ever imagined in a job. I was even given the morning off with pay when Prince Charles and Lady Di came to town, so I could go next door to Queen's Park to see them.

After Ingles House I was in Wilkinson House, a group home for people with psychiatric disorders. It was there, while I was working at the Law Society, when I first reported my stepfather's abuse. I had been seeing Dr. Armstrong for several years. During this time, he told me that I had dissociative identity disorder. He told me that at times during our sessions he was talking to an alter ego of mine who went by a different name and had a completely different persona than my normal one.

That news came as a huge surprise to me. I had no idea I had these alters. My conscious mind was unaware when one of the alters was present. I had never even heard of dissociative identity disorder, or "multiple personality disorder" as it was called at the time. I had to do research on my own to find out more about it.

Dr. Armstrong began treating the disorder with focussing techniques that helped greatly in my recovery. As we worked together, the anger started coming out about the injustices that had occurred. I decided that I needed to put the anger where it belonged instead of putting it on myself. I wanted some accountability from the perpetrator.

Dr. Armstrong gave me the number of a police detective who specialized in cases of sexual abuse. She came over with a tape recorder and got me talking. The investigation began. It was such a relief to finally get it out. The detective believed me, and took the matter seriously. At last! After being doubted and called a liar for so long, I was taken seriously and given a respectful hearing. She assured me that they were going to investigate it. It felt good.

Even so, reporting it must have triggered something else in me, because I apparently called Lorenzo's phone number in North Bay to let him know where I was living. I had remembered the phone number all those years. I had no memory of making the phone call, or of anything that followed. Later on, through Dr. Armstrong's therapy, as my different personalities became integrated, I began to remember being taken to meetings by cult members and being raped and forced to witness various horrors.

On another occasion I phoned Dr. Armstrong and told him I was going to call a cult member. As I was riding the bus on my way to meet the man, I was removed by police officers and brought to the hospital. Dr. Armstrong had notified the police of my whereabouts and told them that I was a danger to myself. I was rescued that time.

As far as my conscious mind was concerned, life carried on as usual, with my work, therapy, and home at Wilkinson House. Even though I loved my job, my attendance was less than perfect. I still became despondent at times and made suicide attempts. This required time off work for hospitalization. I didn't feel comfortable telling my employers the real reasons, so I would ask Dr. Armstrong to write a letter that would be vague as to why I was away and unable to work. Still, when I was at work, I was dedicated, punctual, and hard-working.

After a year at Wilkinson House, I left and moved in with Catherine, a staff member at Ingles House. A single mom and a Christian, she invited me to move in with her and her son. I was very excited about the idea and didn't hesitate to accept the invitation.

A month or two later, I went to visit my mom, who was now living in Halifax. When I arrived, I was shocked and angered to see my grandfather there. I hadn't seen him since the incident in the hotel room. No one else knew about it. I felt so much anger that I wanted to run out of the room. Before I could, his wife said, "Linda, you'd better watch all those fries you're eating at Burger King. If you put on any more weight, you're going to be just like your grandfather."

It was true that I had gained almost forty pounds from all the free food I had been allowed at Burger King. But my step-grandmother's comment set me off. I hated my grandfather for assaulting me, and I told myself, *How dare anyone compare me to him! There is NO way I am ever going to be like him.*

Fuelled by disgust and rage at my grandfather, I immediately began starving myself.

Within five months, my weight dropped from 160 to 100 pounds. My initial goal had been 130 pounds, my ideal weight. But when I reached that target, I still felt fat. I kept on dieting. At 100 pounds, I still saw myself as fat. I kept telling myself "Just five more pounds," but no matter what the scales said, I still looked fat to myself.

Dieting had been easy at the beginning, but the lower my weight dropped, the harder it got. I would starve myself for days without losing much. So I began purging.

Dieting gave me something new to obsess about. Like the drugs and alcohol, dieting was another escape. I couldn't concentrate or think about anything else, because I was constantly focused on my weight. All I could think about was counting calories. It gave me another avenue of control. No matter how much other people bugged me to eat, nobody could make me eat. All my life, I had no control over what happened to me. This was one thing I had one hundred percent control over. No one was going to take it away from me.

While living with Catherine, I began attending church with her and her son every Sunday. I wasn't sure what it was all about. My mind would wander during the services. Even so, I caught bits and pieces of the sermons and worship songs, and started building what I thought was a relationship with Christ. But it was more of an intellectual thing than a heart response. I was confused and didn't understand what it meant to have a personal and intimate relationship with Jesus.

I often heard about how loving God was and would immediately shut down. I hated the word "love." I hated it because I felt so unloved and alone. I felt that I had reached out to God in my darkest hours as a child, and God had forsaken me. I believed that I wasn't good enough for God.

I yearned for somebody to love me the way people in church described God's love, but I had decided that I wasn't worthy of being loved. I couldn't bear the thought of being rejected again, so I covered my longing and fear with anger, and pushed God away.

During this period, even though I was more than content with my job and new home, I was still deeply unhappy. I often thought about suicide, but I didn't want to jeopardize my living situation. I drank heavily, going out to bars after work and coming home drunk. Catherine never said anything, but I'm sure she must have noticed.

Catherine was always good to me. Despite her generosity and kindness, I often lied and stole from her. I didn't need the money; I just took it from her wallet because it was there. She was a disorganized sort of person, so I figured she wouldn't notice anything missing. She never confronted me or questioned me about the missing money, and I never felt remorseful for taking advantage of her.

I got along well with Catherine, but was quite jealous of her son Douglas. It hurt when I saw how she loved him. Irrationally, I wanted her to love me just as much. I yearned for a true family life. In my jealousy, I often lashed out at Douglas, and a kind of sibling rivalry developed between us. The fact that he was ten years younger made no difference to me. The only thing I could see was that he was the competition, standing in my way, depriving me of the attention and affection I wanted so desperately.

I would struggle with bouts of depression, feeling so low without knowing why. I drank to stop those horrible feelings, and turned to food as a way of escape. My anorexia became even more severe. My weight dropped to 82 pounds. I would go days without eating or drinking anything except water. Even water was a problem for me, although I knew it had no calories. Sometimes I would go for three days without drinking anything. I knew that water would edge up the number on the bathroom scale. That was reason enough for me to avoid it.

After starving and dehydrating myself to an unbearable point, I would go on a binge for several days, eating everything I could: two large pizzas, a bucket of ice cream, two bags of cookies, and an entire cake. While I was binging, I was in a different world, dissociated from what I was doing. I felt as though I was eating, but not really eating. Eating was a chore that needed to be completed. There was no pleasure in it. I would swallow all the food as quickly as possible. Then panic would set it, and guilt. I would run to the bathroom to vomit it all up.

I had become quite expert at hiding my eating disorder. I was always alone when I binged. When I was around people and food was involved, I would eat in moderation, so as not to attract attention. I hated those situations and avoided them when I could. Of course, the Christmas season was impossible to avoid. Being a guest at someone's home caused me untold stress and anxiety beforehand. If I knew such an occasion was coming up, I would starve for weeks beforehand. Even then, my alarm would set in after eating a few normal meals. I would pretend to go for a bath or shower, but was actually just running the water to hide the sounds of my purging.

I hated the purging. But my fear of food and gaining weight was greater. Every day I would vow not to binge or purge, but every day I lost the battle. Hunger would drive me to binge, and guilt would drive me to purge. I was trapped in this cycle and couldn't find my way out.

I was so secretive about the issue that I wore double layers of sweat suits to conceal my gauntness. When I went to the doctor's office for a checkup, I tied weight around my ankles in case she decided to weigh me.

People often said when they saw me eating that they wished they could eat like I did and be as thin. It made me angry to hear it. They had no idea what I was going through, and at what a cost my thinness came. I couldn't relax. My mind was obsessed with food and dieting. I had to work continually at keeping my weight down. If I gained a pound, I would freak out and lose two pounds. It wasn't an option not to weigh myself daily. If I went to Nova Scotia to visit my family, I packed my scale. I hated living like this, but the fear of gaining was greater.

I wanted to be able to eat like other people, without terror of putting on weight, but my mind wouldn't let me. I wished I could go back to the days at Burger King, when I ate hamburgers and fries comfortably, but I didn't know how to change my thinking.

SPIRAL

CHAPTER NINE

DURING THIS TIME, MY GRANDMA WAS ALWAYS ON MY MIND FOR SOME reason. I hadn't seen her since she had been carried out of her home by ambulance attendants when I was six years old. I was in my mid-twenties by this point, and I was haunted by thoughts of her. During my sessions with Dr. Armstrong, I often talked about how much I missed her, and how loving she had been. She had left my life so abruptly.

Dr. Armstrong encouraged me to visit her at the Milton District Hospital, where she had been living for almost twenty years. This sounded like a good idea, but I had no transportation, so he drove me there himself, a half-hour's drive from Brampton.

When I walked into her room where she lay in a semi-comatose state, I noticed how skinny she had become. Her hair was now grey, and she had age spots and no teeth. A tracheotomy tube protruded from the base of her throat. Her eyes were open, but glassy and unfocused. No part of her moved except her face, which was quite expressive. She looked perplexed as I approached her, as though she was trying to figure out who I was.

"Hi, Grandma," I said. "I'm Linda, your granddaughter. Nancy's daughter."

She must have understood me, because tears began to roll down her face. I went on to tell her how happy I was to see her, and how much I had been wanting to visit her. Even though she couldn't speak, she was able to nod her head.

I'm not sure how long that first visit was, but when I left I felt excited about having reconnected with her. I came again a few weeks later. This time Cathy, a friend, drove me. I had made applesauce for Grandma, since she could only manage soft foods, and I fed it to her. She smiled at me as she ate. I had purchased a radio for her room so that she could listen to music. I had also made her a big poster with pictures of me and the family.

One of the nurses told me privately how excited the staff was that Grandma finally had a visitor. She said they didn't understand why Grandpa had abandoned her here, that she should have been in a proper care facility rather than a hospital. Apparently Mom had visited a few times over the years, but for the most part Grandma was all alone. She also told me that despite her condition, Grandma was feisty, and gave the nurses a hard time. She hated peas, and if they tried to feed them to her, she would spit them out. I laughed.

I visited Grandma several times, but it was challenging without a car of my own.

Then something happened that changed everything for me.

On one of my trips to visit family in Nova Scotia, I went roller-blading with my fifteen-year-old sister Brit. "Brit" was what we called Brittany. Although I had been initially jealous of her when she was born, after the nurse spoke to me about my attitude, Brit became the love of my life. Protecting her and lavishing love on her had become one of my major focuses.

Brit and I had fun roller-blading in a school parking lot. It was a weekend, so the parking lot was empty. A car pulled into the parking lot and stopped. It was parked there for about five minutes. We were aware of it, but not concerned.

Suddenly, the car backed up and then shot forward at about seventy miles per hour. Before we could even react, it struck Brit.

I couldn't comprehend what had just happened. Brit was lying on the pavement, crying, blood oozing out of her mouth and ear. Her eyes were glazing over. She kept saying, "Linda, I hurt! I hurt!"

I knelt beside her, in shock. Somebody must have called for help, because the next thing I knew an ambulance arrived, lifted Brit onto a board, and sped off toward the hospital. I ran as fast as I could to the hospital, which was five minutes away. I saw Brit hooked up to machines, but she wasn't responding. I went to call Mom.

After an agonizing half-hour wait, a doctor came to tell us that they had done all they could, but she was gone.

I didn't stay around for the funeral. The next day, I flew back to Toronto. I felt guilty and responsible for what had happened and couldn't deal with it.

Why wasn't it me instead? Why didn't I jump in and pull her out of the way? Why didn't I insist she wear a helmet? These thoughts went around and around in my head.

I began drinking even more. I had been living with Catherine and Douglas for two years when the drinking and anorexia began to catch up with me. I became extremely depressed and struggled with concentrating. I had no energy. Simple tasks like taking the dogs for a walk or doing the dishes were too much for me. I couldn't focus on my job.

Dr. Armstrong persuaded me to let him write me a note for work, requesting a leave of absence. I agreed, but when he encouraged me to allow him to tell my employer I was under his care for mental illness, I was hesitant. I was very uncomfortable talking about my struggles with mental health. I had become accustomed to lying to people. Whenever I was hospitalized, I would make up a physical ailment. I didn't think people would understand. They might think I was crazy if they knew the truth. I desperately wanted the people in my life to see me as normal, and not begin to treat me as some sort of leper. My fears were powerful, but Dr. Armstrong managed to convince me that honesty was the best policy.

To my great surprise, my boss seemed most understanding and receptive to my situation. He offered me a short-term disability leave with pay, and encouraged me to take all the time off that I needed.

Initially I was excited at the thought of receiving a paycheque while not having to work. The thrill wore off quickly. I began moping around the house, becoming more depressed than ever. I now had more time than ever to drink and focus on my anorexia. I became isolated. My life felt chaotic and out of control. I was itching to get back to work, counting the days before my disability period was up.

When the time finally came, however, my boss seemed hesitant about my returning. He encouraged me to go on long-term disability. I wasn't interested. Too much idle time was making me crazy. I needed the structure of work to occupy my mind.

When I turned down the idea of long-term disability, my manager informed me that my job had become redundant. He told me there was a position in a different department that I could interview for.

I wasn't upset, because there had been some talk about my job becoming redundant even before I had gone on disability, and I had been assured that I would be given another placement. With that confidence, I went to the interview believing that it was just a formality. To my shock, my manager contacted me later to tell me that I didn't get the job. They were laying me off with a six-month severance package.

I couldn't believe it. I had been promised that my employment was not in jeopardy. No one else was laid off. In fact, people with far less seniority than I had were kept on.

Why was this happening? Despite my struggles, I was a dedicated, hardworking employee, always punctual, and always willing to do not only my own work, but others' as well. I felt betrayed and lied to. My boss had promised me that I wouldn't be laid off. I didn't care about the severance package. I loved my job and just wanted to work.

Yeah right, I thought, thinking of Dr. Armstrong. *Honesty sure is the best policy.*

I thought about challenging my employers' decision, but a lawyer friend advised against it. "There really isn't a whole lot you can do," he said. "Sure, you can claim discrimination, but they'll deny it. Since your job has become redundant, there is no way of proving your claim. By challenging their decision, you'll lose your severance package. And face it, do you really want to work for an employer who wants to let you go?"

This wasn't the advice I wanted to hear, but I knew he was right. I signed the severance agreement and walked away.

I was angry and depressed. I didn't believe that redundancy was the real reason they had let me go. I may not have been the perfect employee, but I had put my heart and soul into the job. I had made a lot of friends there and was never late for work, even though I travelled two hours on transit every morning to get there. At Easter, I would bring a basket of chocolate eggs and bunnies to the office, and at Christmas I bought beautiful gifts for everyone. I was polite and mannerly with everybody, extremely competent, and never refused to help when asked. My performance reviews had always been very positive. Yes, I did take time off two or three times a year because of my depression and suicidal thoughts, but I always had doctor's notes.

Despite my disappointment, I was optimistic and confident that I would get a good reference. With that and my work experience, I was sure I would land another job.

My upbeat attitude was short-lived.

Putting together a good resume and getting interviews wasn't the problem. In the first few months, my phone seemed to always be ringing from some employer interested in meeting with me. The problem was references. I had used my former employer as a reference, sure that he would tell them what a good worker I was. Instead I learned after a few interviews that he was telling inquirers that I struggled with depression and was often "spacey." Potential employers were scared off.

My phone rang less and less often, and then became silent. I was angry and discouraged, deciding that it was pointless to even try. My daily routine consisted of sleeping late, watching TV all day, and going to the bar at night. Drinking made my depression worse, but I was beyond caring. I was losing hope. I had nothing to look ahead to. I questioned my existence, and thought about popping pills, but I liked living with Catherine and Douglas and didn't want to jeopardize that.

Catherine could see that I was struggling. She often approached me to talk and to tell me that she was praying for me. Occasionally I confided in her, but for the most part I remained closed. I couldn't explain to myself what was going on inside. Explaining it to her was impossible.

Then my worst fear came true. Catherine came back after meeting with the pastor at church and asked to speak with me. She said, "Linda, I was just talking with Pastor Dave, and I don't know how to tell you this, but I would like you to leave by the New Year. That will give you two months to find a place. I just feel that Douglas is really struggling and I need to be there for him."

I couldn't believe what I was hearing. I loved living there. Catherine and Douglas were like family to me. How could she do this? Now wasn't the right time, with my severance pay running out and no job. Couldn't she see that? There had to be another solution!

Of course, Douglas had to come first, I thought bitterly. He was her son. I was just a nobody who was in the way. I was furious. I hated Catherine! I hated Douglas! Most of all, I hated God. Pastor Dave had obviously put Catherine up to this. Why had God led Pastor Dave to get Catherine to kick me out?

I spiralled down even further. I had more free time than I knew how to handle. I began drinking on a nightly basis to silence the voices of hopelessness. For the first time ever, I'd had a steady job and stable accommodation, and now it had all vanished before my eyes.

Catherine promised that she would help me find a new place to live. I didn't care. I didn't want to live anywhere else. Instead of expressing how I felt, I sullenly agreed. Catherine could tell I wasn't okay about it, but she assured me that it would work out and we would remain friends.

She kept her promise and found me a one-bedroom basement apartment in a Christian friend's home. Liz was the single mom of a teenage daughter, Angel. I wasn't happy, but it was either move in with Liz or live on the streets. Catherine helped me move, and we hugged each other goodbye.

Liz and Angel seemed really nice, but I had a hard time feeling comfortable. I was shy and struggled with communicating. I had my own bedroom and living room downstairs, but we shared the bathroom, and I had to go upstairs to use their kitchen if I wanted to cook. I was too shy to go upstairs when they were home, but it wasn't a problem, since I preferred not to eat anyway. I had to share the upstairs entrance, which was difficult for me. I knew I was supposed to smoke outside, but I found it so hard to walk by Liz or Angel to go outdoors that I would smoke in the basement instead.

Liz frequently spoke to me about smoking in the house, but I kept on doing it because of my fear of going upstairs when they were home. I'm not sure why, but I was petrified of being around, or communicating with, other people. I preferred to segregate myself from the world around me.

The choices I was making reinforced the negative ideas I had developed about myself. I prostituted my body not because I wanted the money, but because I believed I didn't deserve any better. My body was filth, so why not? I was drowning in addictions because I didn't believe I was capable of anything better, and because they helped me escape my painful thoughts and memories. Whenever anything positive started to happen, I sabotaged myself because I believed I was worthless and undeserving of anything good.

Self-sabotage gave me a sense of control. I would rather be in charge of my own destruction than give someone else that power. Gerry's abuse had made me feel dirty. Being called ugly, stinky, and stupid every day at school had reinforced that belief. I was sure that other people could sense my filth. I couldn't even stand to look at myself in the mirror, so how could I build healthy relationships with others? I was very much alone, with few friends.

I spent my days watching television. My job search was frustrating because I wanted to work in a law office, and my only experience was with a place I couldn't use as a reference. Minimum-wage jobs didn't pay enough to live on. I worried constantly because my severance pay had run out. Unemployment insurance wasn't going to continue forever. I had to figure something out. I knew Liz wouldn't let me stay there for free, and I was afraid to talk to her about my concerns.

Liz and Angel went to church and always invited me to come. I often accepted because it was a chance to get out of the house, but I paid no attention to the sermons.

One day I came home to find that the locks were changed. Liz had become increasingly frightened about the kind of people I hung out with and brought back to my apartment. She was worried about the possible danger to Angel. She left a note on the door, telling me where I could retrieve my belongings.

Once again I was back on the streets. I didn't think I could handle it any longer. More than anything, I just wanted to give up and die. I went to see Dr. Armstrong and told him how I was feeling. He encouraged me to check myself into Mt. Sinai hospital.

This was a novel idea! In the past I had showed up *after* taking an overdose. I went to the hospital and told them I wanted to die. They admitted me to the psychiatric unit. After three or four days there, I told my nurse that I needed to talk to her because I really wanted to die. She said she would talk to me later.

Angered at being put off, I signed myself out on a pass. I stopped at the drugstore and bought three bottles of Tylenol: three hundred pills. I checked myself into a hotel room and washed down the pills with all the beer I found in the minibar.

Lying on the bed, waiting to die, I began to have second thoughts. I was afraid to call the hospital and face possibly being tied down. Instead I phoned Dr. Armstrong and told him what I had done. He promised to call ahead to the hospital, and urged me to go back. When I got there, two security guards were waiting for me, because I was out late on a day pass. They took me back up to the unit. Although Dr. Armstrong had called the nurse on duty to tell them about my overdose, she didn't believe it, and didn't document either his call or my overdose. They simply put me to bed for the night.

Three days later, I felt deathly ill and was vomiting. I told the nurse on duty about the overdose. She notified the doctor on-call, who ordered bloodwork. The bloodwork was inconclusive, because after three days the medication had been ingested by my liver. Within twenty-four hours I crashed and was put on life support.

While there, Sheryl Coffin, the pastor of Rexdale Alliance Church, came to see me. She prayed for God to intervene and heal me. Another pastor, Dave Hearn from Bramalea Alliance, came the next day and prayed over me as well.

The Tylenol had destroyed ninety percent of my liver, and I wasn't expected to survive. When I overhead the staff talking about me outside my ICU, I became very afraid. Even though I had wanted to die, I hadn't really thought about the finality of it, and what it would mean. Deep down, I knew there was a God, even though I didn't understand who that God was. But I did know there was a heaven and a hell. I knew I wasn't ready to face judgment. Terrified, I began to pray. I asked God to forgive me, and promised that if He gave me another chance, I would do everything in my power to get to know Him and give Him full credit for my life.

The hospital contacted my mother in Nova Scotia, and told her I was in the ICU and not expected to live. She came to Toronto immediately to be at my bedside. She brought me a Toblerone chocolate bar, remembering that Toblerone was my favourite. Of course I couldn't eat it because I was so sick, and I remember being angry about it.

All these years she never bought me a Toblerone, and now that I'm dying and can't eat it, she brings me one!

To the doctors' amazement, five days after I had been put on life support, I recovered completely. Nobody could explain how I survived when so much of my liver had been destroyed. I knew God had miraculously healed me. Even so, I was still so angry and stubborn that I reneged on my promise to get to know God and give Him the credit for my being alive.

The hospital released me into my mother's care, and I went to Nova Scotia with her. When she took me to her doctor to follow up on my condition, the doctor asked me how I was feeling. I said that I wished I had succeeded. This landed me back in hospital for another two months.

My mother and I were at odds constantly, as always. We were both very stubborn. She always seemed distant. In her mind, I had always been the problem child, because I was the only one of my siblings who would go head to head with her.

My mom got the bulk of my anger. I should have blamed my abusers most, but I didn't, because I thought that my mother should have protected me. I remember pretty much feeling alone, going to bed and crying myself to sleep, feeling like I didn't have anyone.

One day, during a fight, Mom grabbed me by the arm.

"Don't you ever grab me again!" I yelled. "I'm not that innocent child who can't defend herself anymore."

"I don't know you anymore," she said.

I retorted, "Fine with me. I never knew you for my entire life. A mother is more than a word."

I left and went to spend the night with my dad. While there, I called Dr. Armstrong, who sent me the money on loan to buy a plane ticket back to Toronto. Before I left, I mailed my mother a letter, accusing her of not protecting me and never being there for me. I blamed her for everything that had happened in my life since. I spilled out all my resentment for ten pages, concluding with the words, "A mother is more than a title. From this day forward, I divorce you and do not want to have anything more to do with you in my life."

I flew back to Toronto and spent a few days with a friend until I was able to get a small room at the YWCA on Woodlawn Avenue. The room had a single bed, a small dresser, and a closet. Dr. Armstrong gave me an old television set. There was a community telephone in the hallway, a community bathroom, and a community kitchen.

I don't think I ever used the community kitchen in the two years I lived there. I basically ate out of the vending machines when and if I ate. I often emptied out an entire vending machine at a time for my binges.

I was living on disability, but that wasn't enough to support my drinking habit. I began prostituting myself for drinks and pot, and sometimes heroin. The YWCA was located about two blocks from Dr. Armstrong's office, which made it convenient for me to see him. However, it was only one block from the beer store.

My relationship with Dr. Armstrong was an emotional rollercoaster. My walls were so thick, and my trust so broken, that even his faithful care didn't convince me that he was for real. I challenged him constantly, lashing out at him. I threatened to shoot him, and even stole from him. I continued to try to seduce him. I didn't want a sexual relationship with him; I just wanted to test him, to see if his concern was genuine or not. Amazingly, he never left me.

There were times in Toronto when I was on the streets in minus-thirty temperatures, freezing to death, and I would call him. Even though it was the middle of the night, he would jump in his car and drive forty-five minutes across the city to get me.

Even so, we had a push-pull relationship for years because of my distrust. Had he not stuck with me and gone above and beyond the call of duty, I would never have been able to overcome my fear of intimacy. He convinced me by his behaviour that I had worth and value as a person. He was the closest thing to a father I ever had.

THE TRIAL

CHAPTER TEN

THEY SAY THAT THE WHEELS OF JUSTICE TURN SLOWLY. TWO YEARS after I first reported being sexually assaulted by my stepfather, a preliminary hearing was held at the Mattawa Legion, presided over by a circuit judge. When I went there and gave my testimony, the defence became worried after seeing how articulate and believable I was. They went to my stepfather, suggesting a plea bargain and a trial with just a judge instead of a jury. Gerry refused the plea bargain, but opted for a trial by judge. The case was remanded to trial.

Next the defence went after my hospital records. They were planning to use my psychiatric history against me. If they could cast doubts about my mental stability, it would cast doubt on my whole testimony.

I didn't want all my personal records to be revealed to my stepfather. I felt as though I was the one on trial instead of Gerry. Yes, I had a long history of psychiatric problems, drug addictions, and suicide attempts, along with dissociative disorder, but that was *because* of Gerry! The damage he had done to me shouldn't be used as his defence.

Fortunately, the judge ruled that the defence was only allowed to view my records in the presence of my lawyers. They were not permitted to photocopy my records, but they could make notes from what they read.

Dr. Armstrong and I offered numerous times to make my records available to the Crown Attorney. I thought that the Crown should have as much information as the defence did, in order to prepare their case thoroughly. Instead they brushed aside all my offers. I wasn't happy about it, but I couldn't force them to look at my records.

Several more years went by. Numerous times I was advised of a court date, only to have it adjourned. Then, in April 1983, shortly after I came close to dying in Mt. Sinai Hospital from my Tylenol overdose, the investigating officer, Officer Gardner, contacted me to say that a new trial date had been set for April 1984. I felt both relieved and apprehensive. The trial had already been adjourned five or six times, and I didn't want to get my hopes up.

Both the Crown and the police expressed concerns to Dr. Armstrong that my suicide attempts were a result of pressures surrounding the trial. They thought we should call it off for my sake. I had to convince them that there was no connection between my emotional state and the case, and that I wanted to pursue the matter. I wanted Gerry and Francois to be held accountable for their actions.

Gerry was being charged with having sexual intercourse with a minor under the age of fourteen, and sexual assault on a minor. He was not charged with attempted murder. That was my decision. I thought that by keeping the charges simple, there would be a greater chance of getting a conviction.

Spring arrived the following year, or what passes for spring in the north, and the court case was going to proceed. I had no idea what to expect. I was fairly calm. Naturally, I had some feelings of stress, but Dr. Armstrong assured me that he would go with me. We drove to North Bay together the night before the trial and met with the Crown Attorney at 7:00 in the evening. We brought all my psychiatric records with us to show him. As he read them, he said, "Good grief. I'd better stay up all night and get a handle on this."

The next morning at 9:00 a.m., I walked into the court room with Dr. Armstrong, feeling happy. Six years had gone by between my initial report to the police and this moment. At long last, I was hopefully going to get justice for what Gerry had done to me!

The first day was devoted to Dr. Armstrong's testimony. He gave the court information about my clinical background, my multiple personality disorder, the effects of my emotional trauma that he had been treating over an eleven-year period, the addictions and suicide attempts, the night terrors, the self-destructive behaviours that were a result of Gerry's abuse, and the ritual abuse I had experienced. The ritual abuse was an indirect result of Gerry's behaviour, because if I hadn't told my teacher about my fear of Gerry, Mr. H. wouldn't have used that as an opportunity to bring me to the church in North Bay.

The next day, Tuesday, my mother was put on the stand. I wasn't allowed to be present for that, because I was going to testify later, but I knew that she wasn't there of her own free will. Only a few days before, I had been talking on the phone to my brother Brian, who lived with Mom in Nova Scotia.

"The police were here with a subpoena," Brian told me. "Mom kept saying, 'I'm not going to talk.' They said that if she didn't cooperate, they were going to treat her as a hostile witness and she might go to jail."

That threat and the fear of jail made her come to North Bay and give testimony at the trial. I was in a waiting room when she was on the stand, so I didn't hear her testimony, but I saw her afterward. She showed me her hands. During the questioning, she had dug her nails into her palms so deeply that they left marks.

"I was so nervous," she told me. "I thought they were going to blame me for not protecting you."

I read what she had said in the newspaper later. I was furious when I read that she had told the court she had seen Gerry naked in bed with me numerous times. I remembered her calling me a liar when I had tried to talk about it. She had known it was true all along, had seen it with her own eyes but refused to acknowledge it.

Wednesday was my turn to be questioned—grilled, more like it. For two days, I was interrogated by two defence attorneys whose only goal was to make me look like a liar and a crazy person. During that time, I once again felt as though I was the one on trial. I felt very alone, because I was isolated from the Crown Attorney and investigating officer. They had been my support, preparing me for the trial, but now I wasn't allowed to talk to them.

I was so grateful to have Dr. Armstrong to talk to at the end of each day. There were times when I felt as though I was going to pass out. They would ask the same question ten times in different ways. It was exhausting to go through all that and relive those memories all the while seeing my stepfather sitting right there.

The defence's job was to try to make me look crazy and unbelievable, and they did their best. They were using my life as evidence that I was too unstable to be believed. I felt as though I was being raped and abused all over again. It left me exhausted and wrung out.

The Crown asked me if I had ever disclosed the abuse before. I told them that when I was fourteen, I had disclosed to my Children's Aid worker that I had been sexually abused by my stepfather.

However, when the defence subpoenaed all my records, they found nothing about this disclosure other than the comment, "Linda has a tendency to fantasize about her home life and acts as though she wishes she lived with the Waltons."

I was furious! At the time that my worker wrote that comment, I had bandages on my belly from cutting. I was smashing bottles on my hands and throwing bleach in my eyes. I was running in front of traffic and waking up every night screaming like a terrified animal. Every time I went to sleep, I saw Gerry standing over me with a knife.

At the time, the Children's Aid workers' response was to tell me, "Linda, you better stop it or your parents are going to kick you out."

It was all turned on me like I was just some brat looking for attention. Instead of people trying to figure out my problems and help me, they just labelled me as rebellious. When I was living in a Children's Aid group home for a three-month period, I spent the entire time grounded, with no counselling. Nobody ever asked me what was going on with me. Not until I met Dr. Armstrong did anyone think that maybe there was a reason behind my behaviour.

During the trial, I learned something I wasn't prepared for. The defence asked why I hadn't told anyone at the time, and I said that I had confided in my brother Brian. When they contacted my brother to check, he not only confirmed my statement, but told them that Gerry's brother-in-law Francois had sexually assaulted him as well. When the Crown raised that in court, I was in shock. I'd had no idea! When my brother was growing up, he'd had lots of problems with drugs and alcohol. Then he had developed schizophrenia and became a totally different person. I felt as though the brother I'd known and grown up with wasn't there anymore. But I had known nothing about his abuse at the hands of Francois.

In the end, the judge disallowed the evidence about my brother, because it was new evidence. Even as I was trying to process the news about Brian, I felt let down by the Crown. When I had made my statement to the police years ago, I had told them that I'd confided in my brother. Yet no one had thought to check with Brian in all that time—not until halfway through the trial. So now this information could not be used to help convict Gerry and Francois.

It was a huge relief when that day's questioning was over. The investigating officer told me, "You look so pale." It had been so gruelling that at times I had thought I would faint. But I was determined not to cave.

Next, Gerry and Francois took the stand. They both denied all the charges, although Gerry admitted to hitting me and being in bed naked with me. He stated that it was because my mom wouldn't let him into her bed if he had been drinking. He also said that he saw nothing wrong with being in bed naked with a young girl.

When the Crown Attorney asked Gerry when my birthday was, what my grades in school were, or who my friends were, he couldn't answer.

"So she was just your sex puppet," the Crown said.

But Gerry denied any sexual involvement with me.

When it was Francois' turn on the stand, once again the Crown forgot to introduce key evidence until it was too late. On that last day of the trial, it came up for the first time that Francois already had two previous charges for abusing two of his grandchildren. But the judge would not allow that evidence, since it was introduced so late. In the end, even though I would hope that the disallowed evidence would have indicated his guilt, he was acquitted.

At the end of the two-week trial, the judge adjourned until June 14, at which time he would have his decision. It was a nerve-wracking time, waiting, but I made good use of it.

Throughout the trial, there had been a publication ban on names. The North Bay Nugget covered the trial, identifying me as a "27-year-old woman" and Gerry and Francois as "the complainant's stepfather and his brother-in-law." Because the offenses were of a sexual abuse/assault nature, the newspapers were not allowed to publish my name or the names of the defendants. The idea behind such bans is to protect the victim, but I wasn't ashamed. The ban only protected Gerry and Francois; it didn't protect me. More importantly, I thought that people in their community had a right to know, so that other children in the community would be protected.

"This is wrong!" I complained to Dr. Armstrong. "This ban is like saying that I should be quiet and embarrassed about what happened to me." So he helped me write a formal letter to the Crown Attorney, requesting that the ban be lifted.

In response to my request, the ban was lifted on the last day of the trial.

Gerry was found guilty of sexual assault, but not sexual intercourse with a minor. Because of my past psychiatric history and the lack of hard evidence, the judge couldn't take everything I said at face value, but my mother's testimony and Gerry's admission that he had been in bed naked with me was enough to get him convicted of sexual assault of a minor.

Gerry was sentenced to eighteen months. The judge said that it had been a long time for justice to be served, and that he wanted to give a stiff sentence to send a message that what Gerry had done wasn't okay. I was stunned. Eighteen months was a harsh sentence? I had been given a life sentence!

Even though it wasn't the outcome I was hoping for, it was a relief to be believed after being disbelieved for so many years.

When they led Gerry out of the courtroom, he gave me a long, malevolent glare. I met his eyes and stared him down. I have never felt more empowered. He wouldn't ever again intimidate me or have control over my life.

To say that the trial was a frustrating experience would be an understatement. It felt like a basketball game between the defence and the crown. It didn't seem to be about justice, but about who could sink the most hoops, and who would win. It was definitely worthwhile, but it's not something that everyone could do; it's a tough process. It was all worth it in the end to hear a judge say that he believed me. After years of being called a liar and a rebellious attention-seeker, it was sweet to be believed.

Getting the publication ban lifted was the best part. I had fought a hard fight, and although justice may not have been done perfectly, I felt vindicated. Gerry was not getting off scot-free, and the truth about him and Francois was now known in their community.

A year later, I received more validation in the form of a Criminal Injuries Compensation award of $20,000 for pain and suffering, and another $5,000 for future therapy expenses. This $25,000 was the largest amount allowed under the Criminal Injuries Compensation Act, which indicated that the Compensation Board took my claim seriously.

Although I was happy that I was finally getting justice, of a sort, it didn't mean that I was now happy and recovered. Actually, very little, if anything, had changed.

As soon as I got the money, I began drinking with it. I even began showing up drunk at my appointments with Dr. Armstrong. After that happened a few times, he talked me into checking myself into a detox centre called Women's Own. This was the beginning of a spiral where I became aware that I was an alcoholic, but found the addiction too powerful to break. I would often have a seizure when I stopped drinking. I would stay at detox for a few days, go back to the YWCA to drink, then go back to detox, etc. I was drawn to the detox centre because the staff was so caring. I really began to like them. However, after a few days there, the urge to drink would become overpowering.

I had a grand mal seizure at a detox unit. Scared, the staff called an ambulance. Later, when I was released from the hospital, the supervisor sat down with me and told me that she had never seen anyone experience such a severe seizure. She encouraged me to consider recovery. She was afraid I was going to die otherwise. I was afraid that unless I got away from Toronto once and for all, I would never make it. Still, I wasn't ready to give up drinking.

One time all the beds at Women's Own were full, so I decided to go to a different detox centre. This one was co-ed, and I met some guys there who were crackheads. The next day I signed out with them, and we rented a room and blew my disability cheque on cocaine. This was my first experience with cocaine, and I loved it. Within three hours, we had spent my entire $900 ODSP cheque, and I no longer even had rent money for the YWCA. But I was craving more cocaine, so I gave my credit card and PIN number to one of the guys. We spent the entire night on a crack cocaine run.

Early the next morning, I thought I overhead one of the guys saying he was making me a Kaboom smoke. I didn't know what that was, but I thought it meant they were trying to kill me. I ran outside, dressed only in a t-shirt and underwear, and began running down the middle of the Queensway, waving my arms, trying to flag down a car. I must have been a scary sight. In any case, no one pulled over to help. Eventually I ran inside a 7-Eleven store, begging for help. The store clerk called 911, and the police and ambulance arrived. The ambulance attendant insisted that I go to the hospital because my heart rate was dangerously high. I spent the day at the hospital getting stabilized, then returned to my room at the YWCA.

I was shocked to see that my room was a disaster. My suitcases were cut open, my TV was broken, my clothes were thrown all over the floor. Apparently, when the police decided to check out my story, they made the decision to check out my place. I have no idea what they were searching for.

I stood for a couple of minutes staring at the mess, and then decided to go to the beer store. I bought a case of beer with my credit card and carried it back to my room. I sat on my bed and began drinking. After three beers, the reality of my situation started to sink in. I was completely broke, my rent was due in two days, what little I owned had been de-stroyed by the police, and I now had a credit card bill of $2,000, which was far more than I could ever pay.

I was definitely nearing rock bottom. Even the beer I was drinking didn't taste or feel good. I stopped after the third bottle and decided to go back to Women's Own. I remembered the worker who had told me six months earlier that I needed to get away from Toronto, or I would never make it.

At this point, I started looking at a book that listed different re-covery homes in Ontario. When I read about one called Crossroads in Thunder Bay, I felt a pull. I phoned them, and they invited me to come for an intake interview. A few weeks later, I boarded a bus for Thunder Bay and came to Crossroads.

THUNDER
BAY

CHAPTER ELEVEN

The women's and men's houses at Crossroads Recovery Home were separate, but we all got together for recovery groups. While there, I met a guy named Joe and we became very close friends. He was one of the reasons I stayed so long. We played cards together. He was very spiritual and talked a lot about God and the strength God gave him to recover. I started looking at him as someone who really had his act together. He helped me stay anchored at Crossroads, and I began to believe that everything was going to be okay.

Joe had some friends, a married couple in Devlin outside Fort Francis, who were Christian. The wife, Wanda, would send him lots of Christian poems. I used to read those poems, and they really spoke to me. Wanda later told me that when she heard about me from Joe, she started praying for me on a daily basis. She told me that God would tell her to stop and pray for me many times when she was washing dishes. She would stop whatever she was doing and pray that I would gain control of my life and overcome my addictions. Even though she had never met me, she felt very close to me.

When I had been at Crossroads for seven months, Joe and I got engaged. I told Joe that I was focussed on my recovery, so we wouldn't get married for two to three years. I needed to get off the drugs and alcohol.

Shortly after we got engaged, Joe relapsed. My whole world came to an end. My rock had crumbled. Joe had seemed *so* spiritual, and I had put him on a pedestal, thinking he was the last person on earth who would relapse.

Though I was deeply shaken, I managed to stay on track with my own recovery, with the staff's support. Joe left to go to a recovery home in Kenora. We kept up communication through letters and phone calls and seemed to be doing really well there.

I moved into a three-quarters recovery home and started taking a job readiness program at Confederation College.

Recovery is a slow, step-by-step process. I was regularly seeing a doctor and a therapist from a traumatic stress clinic. I also got involved in the eating disorders program at St. Joseph's Hospital.

It took me a long time to get sick, and I wasn't going to recover overnight. But I was determined to get better. My first goal was not to drink. Once I had managed to stay sober for eight months, my goal became to gain twenty pounds. It was all about small steps, which weren't really that small. I had setbacks, but my counsellors kept encouraging me by pointing out my accomplishments.

Then, out of the blue, Wanda and her husband called me. They told me that Joe was dead. He had been drinking alone, and fell and cracked his skull.

I was stunned. Only the week before, Joe and I had been talking on the phone about how life was good, and about all the things we were going to do after we got married. It made me realize that nobody is invincible.

Heartbroken and shaken, I phoned Frank, one of the counsellors at Crossroads, with the news. He came over right away. Through that difficult time, he continued to visit and console me. Frank became a big support in my life.

After I was raped by another resident at the new recovery place, I dropped out of the college program, became depressed and suicidal again, and was sent back in hospital.

My recovery process was taking a long time. I was sober, but found sobriety to be a place where I felt dead inside. I was hanging on by a wire. I had no purpose, no hope, no career, and no friends. I was full of anger and pain, and didn't know where to go from there. I wondered what I was recovering for, if this was how sobriety felt.

That's when I finally worked up the nerve to phone Wanda. She never pushed me, but kept sending me notes, reminding me that she was praying for me.

I didn't realize it, but besides praying for me themselves, Wanda and her husband had been adding me to countless prayer chains. People I didn't know from all over were praying for me. And Wanda continued to stay in touch even though we'd never met. Every Christmas, she sent me packages.

Frank continued to visit and support me, and eventually we fell in love. Even then, I was lonely and overly dependent on him. Everything was fine as long as he was around, but Frank could only visit me in the evenings after work. During the daytime, I had no college program to keep me occupied and no friends. I felt very isolated. As soon as he was back to work for a day or two, I was in crisis.

I had no life outside of him. I wasn't connected to anything and I had no idea how to be alone without getting depressed. So even with the positive things happening in my life, I still had times, sitting alone in my little apartment on Vickers Street, when I became depressed and suicidal.

One time, when my doctor hospitalized me for depression, a nurse gave me a pamphlet with the Crisis Response number from the Canadian Mental Health Association. She said, "Linda, the next time you feel in crisis, call this number and they'll help."

After that, the next time I was in crisis, I phoned that number and the crisis response mobile team came to my apartment and visited with me. The team consisted of two staff members, who visited me several times and started working with me on some of the issues causing me distress. After addressing several of these issues, Crisis Response referred me to the Rehabilitation Action Program (RAP), run by the Mental Health Association. That team consisted of two staff members, Linda and Shelley, who started working with me, too. They ran the Rehabilitation in the Community program, which was to help people with mental illness stay out of isolation. Isolation and loneliness are huge issues with the mentally ill, often leading to relapse.

The program had two components. The first part involved connecting a client with a volunteer who had similar interests. The volunteer would get together with the client for a minimum six months, meeting with them in the community, going for coffee, dinner, movies, or whatever they enjoyed doing. The second component involved group recreational outings, such as hiking, pizza nights, learning to knit, or scrapbooking—anything fun the group could do together.

I was matched with Bobbi Jo, a young woman I really liked. We loved going to a favourite truck stop where they made an excellent Caesar salad. We also went mini-putting and to the Chippewa Park Zoo. Bobbi Jo was involved with the dragon boat races, and I'd go to root for her team. She was a very down-to-earth person, and I got along great with her.

One Sunday morning, Bobbi Jo came over. We were planning to go to the zoo, but it was raining out. Bobbi Jo was wondering what we should do.

"Why don't we go to church?" I asked.

Bobbi Jo said, "Well, I'm not a church person, but it won't hurt me to go one time."

We drove around a bit, not sure where to go. Then we saw Redwood Park Church. I said, "Let's go there."

I don't think I would have had the courage to go in if Bobbi Jo hadn't been with me.

We quietly sneaked in and slid into the back row. I wanted to get in and out as quickly as I could. I thought I would just listen to the sermon.

All of a sudden, I felt as though I was in another dimension, a dimension of love. God was speaking to me. I had an overwhelming awareness that if I walked away again, I was going to die. I knew that God wanted me right then, that He didn't want me to run anymore. I was exhausted from the battle that was always going on in my head, the drugs and alcohol, and the constant struggle. It was clear to me that God wanted me to drop everything on the floor and say, "Man, I can't do this anymore. I can't run, I can't fight, I just need to give it to you."

What a revelation! My entire life had been one of running and fighting. If I had known how easy it could be not to handle it on my own, I would have done it long ago.

I sat, awed by the awareness of God, of knowing Him, of knowing that Jesus was real! I thought back to when I had made a commitment in

Grade Three, and how I had made a promise to God when I was dying in the Intensive Care Unit at Mount Sinai Hospital.

Oh man, that was God, I thought. *How could I have just turned my back on Him after that? I've been given so many chances, and God's been watching out for me and I didn't realize it!*

For the first time ever, I had a broken and contrite heart. I got down on my knees and bawled my eyes out, feeling a release that was new to me.

Before that moment, I had no hope or purpose. That's why I kept going in these circles. Even in the recovery home, I would wonder what I was recovering for. It makes the recovery very tough when you have nothing to grab onto.

When the service was over, I slipped out quickly and went home without speaking to anyone, but I did fill out a connection card. Bobbi Jo said that she respected my decision but wasn't interested in coming back to church with me again.

Because I had filled out the connection card, Jered, the assistant pastor, phoned me. He was very kind. When I explained a bit about my situation, he put me in touch with a woman named Gini. She came over to my apartment to meet me, and we became instant friends—my first friend at Redwood! She understood me, because she had experienced abuse and struggles in her past as well. That really helped, knowing that I didn't have to be perfect around her. I had always had this sensation that everyone at church was perfect, but I knew Gini could accept me for who I was and where I'd come from.

Gini invited me to attend some Bible studies with her. When I struggled or something wasn't going quite right, I felt comfortable sharing that with her. She was always able to encourage me.

As we continued to meet, God spoke to me about forgiving Gerry. Obviously that wasn't something I felt I could do. But one day, as I was praying, I felt God saying, "Linda, it's okay if you can't forgive him right now, but all I'm asking at this point is that you start praying for him."

I knew that my anger was destroying me inside, so I prayed that God would keep Gerry safe, and that God would help him to experience remorse for his actions. I prayed that he wouldn't victimize anybody else.

I began feeling compassion for Gerry. I thought he must be very lonely. At Christmas time, I prayed that God would put people in his life to share the holidays with.

Over time, as I continued to pray for Gerry, God lifted my anger from me. I realized that God would hold him accountable, so I didn't have to "punish" him with my rage. The only one being punished by my anger was me. Without that burden weighing me down, my life really started moving forward. The past no longer controlled me. Forgiving didn't mean that I had to forget or make myself vulnerable to being abused again. It just meant that I left it with God.

Redwood ran a program called Celebrate Recovery for people who struggled with a variety of issues. That program helped me to realize that despite my past and where I'd come from, I was still very much loved by God and forgiven. I gained a better understanding of the commitment I'd made as a child—that it was about a lifelong personal relationship, not about struggling to be perfect. God knows that I can't be perfect, but that's not what it's about.

I still focussed full-time on my recovery with the eating disorder program at St. Joseph's Hospital, AA meetings, and weekly visits with my doctor. I also went for a six-week program in Guelph called Homewood that helps people deal with post-traumatic stress disorder. I loved it there. It was an excellent program that really grounded me in my recovery. I missed Frank a lot, but he had a surprise waiting for me when I came home at Christmas. When I opened my stocking, I found an engagement ring in the bottom! So Frank and I got engaged in December 2001.

My excitement was short-lived. When I sent wedding invitations to my family, no one responded, except for Aunt Lois and Uncle Bill who sent a card with a cheque. No one else called or sent so much as a card. No one from my family attended. I had been planning a church wedding at Redwood, but after that, our plans quickly changed. I couldn't handle having a church wedding with nobody from my family there.

I hadn't spoken to my mom since I had written her that letter, divorcing her. Still, I thought she would be happy for me and want to share in my big day. I thought that maybe she couldn't afford to travel to Thunder Bay for the wedding, so I phoned her and offered to come to Nova

Scotia to get married. All she said was, "I checked out all the hotels and there's nothing available here for you to stay at."

I had phoned my dad, who was living in Alberta after separating from Beatrice, and he promised to come. But in June, two months before the August wedding, I tried to call and discovered that his phone was disconnected. Nobody seemed to know how to contact him. He never came to the wedding, and I never heard from him again.

Frank and I were married in August 2002 by a justice of the peace. Wanda came, along with Bobbi Jo, and Don and Ruth, good friends from Toronto. We all went out to a Chinese buffet for supper afterward.

We had a brief honeymoon in Toronto. We did the tourist thing, shopping and going up the CN Tower. When we returned home, we moved into Frank's apartment.

It felt surreal being a newlywed. I no longer had the stress of coping alone or the fear of ending up homeless. It had always been my dream to be married, but I had never believed my dream would come true. It was a very happy time.

I was at home, learning to cook and volunteering with the Canadian Mental Health Association. They had helped me so much. They made me feel good, and were sensitive towards me. Giving back by volunteering seemed the natural next step.

I had always felt like a burden on society. I hadn't known I had anything to give until I started volunteering. The experience changed my life. It worked for me almost like medication, but without the side effects.

At first I did the one-on-one matchups, just as Bobbi Jo had done with me. Eventually I switched to group recreation events, helping out with movie nights, hikes, game nights, an annual picnic at Sibley Park, a monthly breakfast club, a walking club, basketball, bowling, mini-putt, bocce, and lots of other activities. The focus was on having fun and socializing, not talking about mental health issues. Getting out in public and having a good time wasn't an experience many of us had been accustomed to.

Being able to volunteer and do things to help people gave me purpose and kept my spirits up. My self-esteem improved.

A month after Frank and I were married, Joanne Books from the CMHA approached me to share my story on behalf of the United Way.

I had never thought about public speaking or telling my story. As I considered it, I began thinking that maybe I did have a story to tell. The idea scared me, but I agreed to do it.

My first speaking date was for provincial government employees at the Valhalla Inn in Thunder Bay. It was a nerve-wracking experience, standing up and telling my story in front of all those people. I read into the microphone from my notes, cramming my life story into ten minutes. My heart was pounding a mile a minute.

I got a standing ovation. All kinds of people came up to me after and expressed their appreciation. I just felt relieved it was all over.

The positive response encouraged me to continue doing speaking engagements. That fall, I spoke thirty times in a three-month period. Within two months, the local newspapers and CBC Radio began interviewing me, and more speaking invitations followed.

On one of those occasions, I spoke to a class of child and youth workers at Confederation College. The teacher had invited me to share my story with the students. Afterwards, one girl came up to me in private and said that she had been planning to take her own life. After hearing my story, she changed her mind! I was beyond thrilled and grateful that I could make that kind of difference. It motivated me all the more to keep telling my story.

On another occasion, one of the pastors at Redwood interviewed me at church in front of the congregation. Afterward, a man came to tell me, "I've never been to church before. This was the first time in my life. I just moved to Thunder Bay, into Crossroads. I'm struggling with addictions. This morning, I felt I needed to come to church. You inspired me to keep going."

I could hardly believe it. It gave me chills to think that he was in the same recovery home I had been in when I first came to Redwood and encountered God. It was obvious to me that God was using me to help other people.

In January, Linda Gluck, a staff person at the CMHA, phoned to ask if it would be okay if she nominated me for the Courage to Come Back Award, a provincial award given by the Centre for Addiction and Mental Health (CAMH). I agreed, not really expecting anything to come of it. The CAMH receives numerous applications for the annual award, so I was stunned when they called me in March to say that I was one of the seven recipients that year, along with Ontario's then-Lieutenant-Governor James Bartleman!

I was in disbelief. I didn't think I matched up with the other recipients—the Lieutenant-Governor; Dan Carter, a television host from Oshawa; and former Toronto Maple Leaf Ron Ellis among them. I felt way out of my league.

As soon as word got out, I was inundated with calls and media requests for interviews. It was hard for me to handle all this attention. I had never set out to volunteer for the recognition.

I found out about my award in March, and the award ceremony was in May, at a gala dinner in Toronto. I was allowed to bring four guests. Frank and Linda Gluck were my Thunder Bay guests, and I was delighted to invite Dr. Armstrong and his wife from Toronto. Of all people, I wanted to share this moment with Dr. Armstrong, who had stayed with me unswervingly over twenty years, no matter how difficult I made it for him.

Dr. Armstrong was as excited and proud as a father coming to his daughter's graduation. We were treated to a gala at the Westin Harbour Castle Conference Centre, sponsored by RBC Capital Markets. The Honourable Michael Wilson, former Minister of Finance, attended.

I sat at a table with executives from BMO Financial, the sponsors of my award. I still couldn't believe that I was winning the award along with all these amazing people.

When I was given my award, I made a brief speech:

First of all, I would like to thank the Centre for Addiction and Mental Health; my sponsor, BMO Financial; and all those who have made this evening and award possible for me.

To be honest, I feel a bit uncomfortable receiving this award in the sense that I feel that I absolutely love what I'm doing by being able to inspire and touch so many people's lives and that I'm being rewarded for what I have such a passion for doing.

It was such an honour for me to just be nominated by knowing that so many people in my community felt I deserved to be recognized for what I was doing, that I never dreamt in a million years that I would actually win this thing. I feel like I've been in this never-ending dream over these past couple of months that I just won't wake up from.

I feel this award really is a joint effort, as there have been numerous people that have helped me during my journey towards recovery.

First, I would like to thank God, who has been the backbone to my strength over these past few years.

Secondly, I would like to thank my ex-psychiatrist Dr. Harvey Armstrong, for being there and not giving up on me. You went way beyond the call of duty with me. I thank you so much for believing in me enough to help keep me alive until I was able to find enough purpose and reason to keep myself alive.

Thirdly, I would like to thank the Canadian Mental Health Association (Thunder Bay Branch) and especially Linda Gluck and the Rehabilitation Action Program for nominating me for this award.

The C.M.H.A. has been there for me right from the beginning of my recovery journey and has provided me with the tools, healthy soil, and the opportunities to get where I am right now, and I also believe I would not be here today if they had not been there for me.

Finally, I would like to thank my loving husband, Frank. You have also really been there for me. I thank you for all of your love and support towards me and I would not have been able to accomplish everything that I have without you.

I would like to challenge everyone here this evening. The next time you run into someone who is struggling with addictions or appears to be suffering from mental illness, please don't be so quick to judge them.

The chances are that person has a story similar to mine or one of the other stories here tonight. Unless you have been there, you can't possibly understand the loneliness and darkness that comes with addictions and suffering from mental illness.

If you are feeling a bit courageous, I challenge you to offer this person a handshake or a friendly word of encouragement or smile, because something so simple can go a really long way in someone's life.

Thank you all.

During the media blitz that followed, I received a flood of speaking invitations. That led to my appearance on the Christian talk show *100 Huntley Street* in September 2009.

But in the meantime, I had another challenge to face.

LONGING FOR CHILDREN

CHAPTER TWELVE

WHEN FRANK AND I GOT MARRIED IN 2002, I IMMEDIATELY BEGAN trying to get pregnant. I loved kids and couldn't wait to have a child. At the same time, I suffered from severe endometriosis, which was blocking my fallopian tubes. I was menstruating twenty-eight days a month and suffering from severe pain that made it feel like I was being stabbed.

At all times I was focusing on two things: my desire for a baby, and the pain of the endometriosis. I went through seven different surgeries to unblock my tubes, until my doctor finally told me that my only hope of pregnancy was through in vitro fertilization, a very expensive process.

I became obsessed with saving enough money for the procedure, and got upset with Frank if we spent a penny on anything that I thought was unnecessary. Our computer broke down and our car needed repairs, but I insisted that we couldn't spend the money on either of those things.

Frank didn't share my passion for kids, because he already had an adult son from a previous marriage. He was quite content to have a childless marriage with me, and didn't understand why I was so consumed with this. It caused a lot of stress between us.

One Sunday morning when we were at church, the youth pastor's wife was invited onto the stage to share her story. She brought her young son with her, and told us about how she had struggled for years with infertility. I listened, sensing God speaking to me through her words.

She said that when she finally surrendered her desire for a child to God, she became pregnant.

When I came home, I got on my knees and gave it all to God. Immediately I felt a deep, real peace. I also sensed God saying to me, "If you really mean it, take the money you've saved, let Frank get a new car, and donate the rest of it. Then I want you to take it one step further and have a hysterectomy."

I did.

Three months later, Frank said, "Why don't we foster kids?" That sounded good to me, so we went through the application process. Two weeks later, Children's Aid called to say, "We have a newborn baby for you to foster." That was how Matthew came to us. He was five days old.

We loved Matthew, but his biological father made things a nightmare. Matthew had colic and cried for six hours every night. We walked the floors with him, night after night. However, his father refused to allow us to take the baby to the doctor. Matthew had to go three times a week for supervised visits with his father, who kept looking for things to complain about his care. It felt to us as though it was more about control than concern.

Matthew's mother said very little. She obviously missed him. But Children's Aid obviously felt that they weren't able to care for him adequately, because within that first year it became clear that he was going to become adoptable. We expressed our interest to the Children's Aid Society, and they agreed to support us in that desire.

A year and a half later, at two and a half, Matthew became ours, which we celebrated with a big drop-in party and cake. We have kept up that tradition every year since on his adoption day.

Just before Matthew's adoption was finalized, Children's Aid informed us that his biological mother had become pregnant again. They asked if we would be willing to foster the new baby if it became necessary. We were so excited at the possibility that we began buying new things for the baby. Later, the agency changed its mind and decided to give the mother a second chance. We were very disappointed and confused. We had been given Matthew because the mother didn't have the capacity to care for a child. Why would that be different with a new baby?

Two years went by. Then, out of the blue, Children's Aid called to ask us if we would foster Brayden. We agreed immediately, and within two hours they brought him over.

He was a sad sight. At two and a half, he had no shoes, no diapers, no bottles, and wore ill-fitting clothes. He couldn't express anything. He seemed lifeless. He never cried or fussed. If I put him down, he didn't move from the spot. It broke my heart.

He bonded with Frank immediately and took a big liking to Matt. They became instantly joined at the hip. However, he pulled away from me. It was hard for me, but I understood that he was going through a lot.

That first night was sad. As I tucked him into bed, his eyes were glazed and he kept saying, "Mom, Mom, Mom." All I could do was hug him.

As time went on, it became clear that he couldn't or wouldn't express his feelings. If he got hurt, he wouldn't cry. If he was angry, he wouldn't tantrum. One time, when he was in bed, there was a thunderstorm. I thought he might be scared, so I went into his room to check on him. He was sitting up in bed, tears rolling down his face. He didn't make a sound.

It took lots of work and assurance on our part to convince him that it was okay to express himself. You'd never know it today! He's the first one to throw tantrums and express himself.

Over time, with patience, I won him over, and he loves Frank and me equally now.

Children's Aid asked us right from the time Brayden came to us if we would adopt him. We agreed, but it was a long process. The father fought the adoption, and we had to go through the courts. Finally, the day before we were to sign the adoption papers, the father put in a last-minute appeal. He didn't follow through on the appeal, but it still delayed things for another year. Brayden was almost four when the adoption went through.

We always celebrate the boys' adoption days—their "second birthdays"—every year. It's a big deal in our home, and the boys get very excited about it.

RECONCILIATION

CHAPTER THIRTEEN

When Matthew was two years old, before Brayden came to us, I got an email from my brother Doug in Nova Scotia: "Linda, please contact me asap. It's urgent."

I hadn't had any contact with my family in years. The last time I had communicated with any of them was to invite them to my wedding.

Worried, I phoned him right away.

"It's Brian," Doug told me. He went on to tell me that Brian had been taken ill a few days before, and had died the night before.

I didn't understand at first. All that registered was that Brian was ill. When I realized that my brother Brian, who had been my best friend and closest ally, was gone, I went into shock. Brian, who had been my childhood confidante, who had told me, "Don't worry, we're in this together. I've got your back."

Brian had died of a brain aneurism. My mind went back to the conversation we had as children about Grandma's aneurism. Brian had said then that if the same thing ever happened to him, he wouldn't want anyone to operate on him; he would prefer to die. True to his word, he had been offered surgery at the time he took ill, but turned it down. He got his wish.

I decided to go to Nova Scotia for the funeral. That might seem like an obvious decision, but for me it wasn't an easy one to make. After divorcing my mother and being estranged from my family for so long, I wasn't comfortable about facing them all, especially at such a time.

Frank and I arranged babysitting for Matthew and flew to Nova Scotia in time for the visitation at the funeral home. Brian was in an open casket. He was only thirty-eight years old. It was unbearable to see him there. Of all my siblings, he had been the closest to me.

My mother had flown in from California, and was talking and laughing with people in the room. She didn't speak to me or acknowledge my presence. My discomfort grew, and I became very angry at the way she was talking about her flight and how great life in California was. I wondered how she could act as though this was a happy reunion and show no emotion about her son's death.

At the same time, I wanted to talk to her, but I didn't feel this was the place to risk a scene, so we ignored each other. It takes a lot of energy to ignore someone, especially when you're already in turmoil.

At the funeral the next day, Doug spoke on behalf of the family. He talked about climbing trees with Brian, and about Brian teaching him how to ride a bike. Doug didn't get too far before he broke down.

After the funeral, the minister came up to me and said, "I understand you're from out of town. Your brother Brian talked so much about you. He thought very highly of you. He attended my church and often sang solos. He was scheduled to be baptized in two weeks. I want you to know that he very much knew Jesus."

That made my day. I had no idea that Brian had come to faith. What a peace that minister gave me! Even though I had lost my brother, I would see him again in heaven.

At the graveside, for the first time, my mother's composure broke. As they began to lower the casket into the ground, she grabbed the coffin and began freaking out. My heart went out to her when I saw how broken she was.

Oh my gosh, I thought *She really does care!*

I couldn't hold back. I went up to her, gave her a big hug, and said, "Mom, the past is the past."

She clung to me. In that moment, I realized how precious life is. We never know when our time will come, so it makes no sense to hang on to grudges and resentments. Carrying all that bitterness and anger inside hadn't done me any good.

Since that moment, my relationship with my mom has been totally different. No matter what she's done or not done, she's still my mother and we have always loved each other.

Once the ice was broken between us, Mom asked for pictures of my family. She hadn't even known that Matthew existed until she'd overheard me talking about him.

Over the next several days, I reconnected with my relatives. That's when I learned that my dad was very ill. My half-sister Amber in Alberta had contacted the funeral home to explain that Dad was recovering from major surgery and that's why he had been unable to attend Brian's funeral.

Despite my grief, I was ecstatic about reconciling with my mom. This time, we parted on really good terms, which was a great feeling. A week later, she emailed me:

Our talking again at Brian's funeral was an answer to prayer. It made me feel that Brian didn't die in vain. His death had a purpose. It brought us back together.

That email helped me to understand that I really did matter to my mother. All my life, I had felt like she didn't care, but it was just that she had a hard time expressing her feelings. I thought back to when I was dying in the hospital and she had brought me a Toblerone bar. The gesture had angered me at the time, but I saw it now in a new light. She had been trying in her own way to demonstrate love.

I think that because she had been going through so much in her own life, she couldn't show her affection. Now that I understand, she and I have been working to build our relationship. She has become a wonderful grandmother to my boys, and very supportive of me. As always, she doesn't want to talk about the past. I accept that. It's the present and the future that's important.

Even so, knowing from my own experience how much I longed for affection as a child, I make sure that my boys hear many times a day how much we love them.

Over the next few years, I tried to track down my dad. Even though Amber had contacted the funeral home with his regrets, nobody in the family seemed to know where he was living in Alberta. Every few weeks, I Googled funeral homes and obituaries in Alberta, but I didn't see his name. I hadn't heard from him since the time he had promised to come to my wedding to give me away.

One day, as I was scrolling through Calgary obituaries, I saw a notice about my father's death. In the list of surviving family members, all his children were mentioned, except for me. I contacted my sister Katy in Nova Scotia, because she was Facebook friends with Amber. Amber confirmed that Dad had died. She had apparently not thought it necessary to let his other family know.

I felt a mixture of emotions. I felt sad and empty, because a piece of me had died. I felt my trust betrayed all over again. I was angry, too, thinking of how my life might have turned out differently if he hadn't left us. At the same time, there was a sense of relief that I didn't have to hold on to him anymore. I could move forward.

AN UNEXPECTED CHALLENGE

CHAPTER FOURTEEN

"Linda, you have cancer."

The voice on the phone was my family doctor's. Frank was out of town on a fishing trip, out of reach by phone. The boys were away at summer camp. I was alone in the apartment.

My first thought was, *Oh my gosh, I'm going to die!*

The doctor's voice continued, trying to be reassuring, but all I felt was panic. After she hung up, I got on my knees, and said, "Oh, God, I don't understand this. It's so scary!"

Thoughts of my boys played over and over in my head. I wasn't afraid of death. Jesus had taken care of that. But the thought of leaving my boys without their mom was unbearable.

In the midst of my panic, I sensed God saying, "Linda, trust me." It was really hard to do, but I decided to pray that God would use this new journey to help others.

I had just stepped down after serving a three-year term as chair of the local Canadian Mental Health Association, and I was looking forward to all the free time ahead. I hadn't foreseen that my time would be taken up in quite this way!

I couldn't sit on this information. I needed somebody to talk to, so I posted my news on Facebook. The outpouring of support I got helped me through the next five days as I waited for Frank to return home. Friends called, visited, and prayed. Still, it was hard being alone. I paced in my apartment and visualized telling Matthew and Brayden the news. Imagining it would start me crying.

The only people in my extended family who had suffered from cancer had died from it. I went to the internet to research the disease, but it wasn't all that helpful, since I had no idea even what stage my cancer was at.

Since there was no way to contact Frank, I just had to wait for his return. Five days later, he seemed very unresponsive to my bombshell. He just said, "It'll be okay," without much apparent emotion.

I was angry at his calmness, as though I had told him about a flat tire or something equally trivial. Illogically, I was also angry at him for being away on a fishing trip, even though I had been completely supportive of his going. I didn't realize that he needed time to process his shock. A few days later, he began opening up and comforting me, saying, "It'll be okay. We need to pray." This time when he said, "It'll be okay," it sounded more heartfelt.

We picked up Matthew and Brayden after their summer camp and told them the news at home. Matthew started crying, and Brayden followed suit. I lost my composure and began reassuring them, saying, "It's okay. Mommy's not going anywhere."

I couldn't bear to see them so upset.

On August 23, the week before my scheduled lumpectomy, I posted this message on Facebook:

I honestly have a whole new admiration for those who have been diagnosed with cancer, especially those who are terminally ill. I truly have a lot of confidence that my cancer has been diagnosed early and that my surgery next week will confirm an early diagnoses. However, it is still very very scary. I feel that I truly have to dig deep inside for the courage right now, which I know is there and I am so thankful for the numerous family and friends I have that are praying for me and are there for me to help me get through this tough time in my life. I honestly know that I will grow even more as a person after getting through this tough challenge in my life. I am honestly not looking forward to the surgery I am having next week, but at the same time I am very confident in knowing that my God is the Master of all Physicians and will be there right beside me during the whole time and will be guiding the surgeons, radiologist, and nurses. I will courageously continue to move forward, trusting in my God and continue rejoicing in my Lord because my God is an awesome God!!!

Fortunately, things moved quickly. Two weeks after the surgery, my doctor phoned to tell me that the results were good. The cancer appeared to be at Stage One, with no apparent spreading.

I started to relax and our family celebrated that evening.

The oncologist recommended that as soon as I healed from the surgery, I should go for radiation treatments as a precaution. I was apprehensive but agreed. Even though I was less fearful, knowing that I was at Stage One, the whole experience was overwhelming. Each time I went for treatment, I'd think, *Wow, I can't believe I'm really here in the cancer clinic. The doctors must have made a mistake.* Maybe I was still somewhat in shock.

Every time I came for treatments, I would see other patients waiting. Over time, they began to feel like family and friends. I talked to people whose cancers were at Stages Three and Four. Seeing their strength and courage amazed me. It was uplifting and encouraging. At the same time, it was hard to think that they were nearing the ends of their journeys.

Initially, I was able to be upbeat about my own journey. On November 17, I posted:

Heading out soon for day 3 of radiation treatment. Soon, there will only be 13 more to go!!! After my radiation treatment I'm going to Bombardier with the United Way to speak to about 300 employees between 2 different speaking engagements. I love how despite being diagnosed with cancer and being in treatment, God continuously is showing me that he still has a plan for my life and continues to provide opportunities for me to be able to make a difference in other people's lives! My God is an awesome God!!!

I tried hard to stay positive, but it was tough when my skin started burning and I was growing increasingly tired as a result of the radiation.

Each time I'd come in and say, "I'm here for my spa treatment." The nurses would laugh.

My November 28 post showed my brave front starting to crack:

Day 12 DONE! Very thankful that Frank has not asked for a divorce and my boys have not asked for a new mommy yet! because I have been quite the bear this week! My patience has seemed to completely disappeared on my! Staring at this messy house and pile of laundry that needs to be done, sure ain't helping with my mood right now. I think I'm just feeling sorry for myself, and need to give myself a shake to snap out of it. 4 more days to go!!! And the amazing thing is that my God is an awesome God and He still loves me despite all my weaknesses and faults!

On December 2, I was nearing the end of my treatments, and also the end of my endurance.

Day 14 DONE! 2 more days to go!!! I have to be honest that I am dealing with quite the tomato radiation burn, which is very sore and I am still very lethargic and it is very hard to pump myself up about the idea of going into the hospital to get more radiation when it is the radiation that is causing these symptoms.

The next day, when I went for my second last treatment, I noticed a metal triangle with a metal stick attached. I asked the nurse what it was for, and she said that whenever someone completed their course of treatments, they would hit the triangle as hard as they could with the stick to let everyone know. I couldn't wait!

On December 4, I posted this on Facebook:

Day 16 DONE!!! O more days to go!!! That is zilch, nada, nil. I rang that bell loud and proudly when leaving the radiation department for my final treatment today. I was even given an Award of Excellence certificate that certify's that I have completed my prescribed radiation treatments with high honours in courage,

cooperation and good spirits, signed by all the radiation thera-
pists. I think I will proudly display this certificate on my wall as it
was definitely the toughest one in my life to earn! And I definitely
could not have completed my treatments without my God because
on the days I felt that I did not have the strength or energy to go in
for my treatment my God filled me with His strength and carried
me because my God is an awesome God!!!

I am hoping for the best, since my cancer was caught early. I learned
a lot about the cancer experience that I didn't know before.

In the past, when people I knew faced that battle, I tried to be understanding and supportive, but I couldn't identify with the fear. I get it
now. I appreciate what a courageous battle it is, with all the appointments
and treatments involved. I have a whole new admiration for people who
go through it.

TODAY

CHAPTER FIFTEEN

It was a quiet, peaceful evening before Christmas. Frank was out shopping with our son Matthew. I was at home, working on the computer while seven-year-old Brayden sat at the kitchen table, busily making Christmas cards.

"Here, Mommy." Brayden had come over to my side and was offering me an envelope addressed "To Mommy and Daddy." Too excited to wait for Frank to get back, he wanted me to open it right away.

I pulled out the card, with a picture on the front of a Christmas tree and a person standing beside it. The words "Merry Christmas to You" were printed above the tree. Inside the card were the words "Santa is giving out gifts. I love you." A five-dollar bill was enclosed.

I was surprised and touched—not just because it was unexpected, but because I knew this was all the money Brayden had left from his allowance.

My first impulse was to hand the money back to him and say, "Honey, thank you very much, but you don't need to give us your money." But I sensed that this was too important a moment to dismiss. I have always prayed that Brayden would grow up to have a giving heart toward others. It would be wrong to reject his generosity now.

I asked him, "Brayden, are you sure you want to give this to Mommy and Daddy?"

His answer astounded me. "Yes, Mommy. You and Daddy have given me so much in my life by adopting me and giving me my food and clothes. I want to show you how much I love you."

Choking up, I gave him a big hug and thanked him.

"Why are you crying?" he asked.

"Oh, these are happy tears. I'm just so happy that you love us."

The next day, I bought him Timbits, his favourite treat which he usually paid for with his allowance.

Brayden's nine-year-old brother Matthew is a gem as well. He loves to make my bed for me, leaving notes on it that read "Mom, this bed was especially made by Matthew."

He knows how to get around me with his unique way of reasoning. I remember a conversation with him at the grocery store. He was pestering me to buy ice cream. I said, "How can you eat ice cream in February when it's so cold outside?" He promptly answered, "We just learned about the law of probability in math class, and it's very probable, if I open my mouth and put ice cream inside, that I could eat it." I bought the ice cream.

Both boys love to help others and pay it forward. When a part of our city was severely damaged by flooding in 2012, we visited some of the homes to bring sandwiches and see how we could help. Matthew and Brayden met a boy around their age who had no clothes other than what he was wearing, because his bedroom was destroyed by the flood. They were so moved that they decided to donate their spring jackets to help him out.

I am a blessed woman. Between my two amazing sons and my quiet, devoted husband Frank, my life overflows with love. Next to spending time with my boys, my favourite thing is volunteering. I love being put in situations where I can make a difference and help out, whether by babysitting for a friend, serving at my church, or speaking for the United Way and the Canadian Mental Health Association.

We have opted for a simple lifestyle, so that I can stay home and spend every possible moment participating in our sons' lives. I know from personal experience how important a child's memories are in forming the person he or she becomes. Because of that, I am passionately committed to building happy memories for our boys!

Our apartment is simply decorated with family photos on the wall, a cat tree by the window so our cat Cutie can enjoy the view, and my prized possession, a Patrick Sharp jersey, framed and hung over the couch. I also love the Toronto Blue Jays, the Chicago Blackhawks, pizza, and movies, but there is no joy that compares with helping people. It's my way of showing gratitude to God for what He rescued me from, and how much love He has lavished on me.

On the bookshelf in the living room is my award: a glass sculpture shaped like a book with open pages. I received it in 2004 from the Centre of Addiction and Mental Health. On the front is etched these words

The Courage to Come Back Award recognizes and honours people across Ontario who have displayed courage and determination in the face of adversity. The award formed from glass symbolizes how vulnerable and fragile the human spirit can be, yet when framed with courage and dignity, it is inspiring in its strength and beauty.

This is my story. It is my heartfelt prayer that it will bring hope to many who have suffered from abuse and addiction.

VISIT THE AUTHOR AT
WWW.MARIANNEJONES.CA

Brayden's Adoption Day

Lightning Source UK Ltd.
Milton Keynes UK
UKOW06f1001051215

264045UK00011B/209/P